Bold and per society; search in its challenge to the church. This is an outstanding and highly readable book which will serve to equip Christians for effective living in today's world.

William Taylor
Rector St Helen Bishopsgate,
London

Alien Nation

Melvin Tinker

Christian Focus

© Melvin Tinker
ISBN 1-85792-677-3

First published in 2001
by
Christian Focus Publications, Geanies House, Fearn,
Ross-shire, IV20 1TW, Scotland, Great Britain
www. christianfocus. com
Cover design by Alister MacInnes

Contents

For Dave and Jan
Who were right all along.

Foreword

The patrons of the 'Dog and Duck' are happy enough with page three of the Sun now moved to page one – but the 'political correctness' of Islington leaves them cold. They are strongly in favour of capital punishment, against foreigners of all kinds and think that there should be police on the streets to give the uncontrollable kids a clip round the ear. As for their views on single sex marriages....!

What Christians have in common with the pundits of the 'Dog and Duck' is a belief in right and wrong, crime and punishment, which is missing from the pundits of our intellectual elite. Both of us feel that our society is being systematically destroyed; but we Christians also believe that, as the 'salt of the earth', it is up to us to do something about it.

But as we try to engage on the issues, we find the goalposts constantly moved. The need to preserve the health and life of a pregnant woman turns into a woman's right to choose. The right of people to do what they like between themselves in private turns into a demand that what they do is affirmed by society. When the church tries to draw a line in the sand, it is told that it has no legitimate voice in a multi-faith society.

While the statistics of social disaster mount, our intellectual elite is in denial. What has happened, and what can we do to turn the tide?

Melvin Tinker's book gives us answers, which are rooted both in the Bible and in society as it is. As vicar of a large and growing church in the city of Hull, he lives in both worlds.

He tells us what instinctively we know, but do not like to admit, that society is sliding into paganism at a breathtaking speed, that we live in a latter-day Babylon, not in the secular humanist society of our intellectual leaders. The net effect of all their talk is to dismantle civilization.

His way back is to look again at each of the biblical foundations with a particular emphasis on the family, which is the cornerstone of every society, every religion and every culture in recorded history. Yet soon, half our children will grow up without two parents committed to each other and to them. Marriage is the first institution made by God and we cannot water down or reconstruct that lifelong commitment.

Deprived of reasoning and rational faith, people have turned back to pagan gods. It is not just the annual Glastonbury festival, it is the fetishes sold in shops in cathedral cities and the horoscopes in the daily papers, by which people now order their lives.

Melvin Tinker shows how Christian teaching deals with this moral darkness. He looks at the basis of our new secular society – materialism, individualism, hedonism, relativism and the counter-culture, and the promise that despite all, God is still with his people. It is the Babylon captivity. As the old Babylon disappeared, so will the new. And, exposing the glaring flaws in each new 'ism', he gives the powerful biblical basis of the Christian position, the line at which we have to stand and fight.

Melvin has that rare capacity both to get under the skin of our modern Babylon and also to expound the key passages in the Bible which show up its errors then and now, and to encourage us to stand firmly by what is right and good and true.

This is no academic book, written in the library far away from the pressures of life. It bears all the marks of being delivered from the pulpit to a congregation who live in the middle of terraced houses and flats in which human struggles and tragedies take place. What is more, it grips the reader as the preacher has to grip the audience.

But, above all, it is a realistic matching of the Babylon of the old to the Babylon of today. God's people survived the first Babylon, overthrown after seventy years of captivity. They survived the new Babylon of Rome, when it was overthrown. More recently, they have survived Fascism, which cost fifty million lives, and seventy years of

Communism. This book gives us courage to stand for what is right, good and true without flinching, and to win hearts as well as minds by showing selfless love in a selfish society.

Sir Fred Catherwood,
President of the Evangelical Alliance

Chapter 1

By the Rivers of Babylon

Psalm 137

¹By the rivers of Babylon we sat and wept
    when we remembered Zion.
²There on the poplars
    we hung our harps,
³for there our captors asked us for songs,
    our tormentors demanded songs of joy;
    they said, 'Sing us one of the songs of Zion!'

⁴How can we sing the songs of the Lord
    while in a foreign land?
⁵If I forget you, O Jerusalem,
    may my right hand forget its skill.
⁶May my tongue cling to the roof of my mouth
    if I do not remember you,
if I do not consider Jerusalem
    my highest joy.

⁷Remember, O Lord, what the Edomites did
    on the day Jerusalem fell.
'Tear it down,' they cried,
    'tear it down to its foundations!'

⁸O Daughter of Babylon, doomed to destruction,
    happy is he who repays you
    for what you have done to us –
⁹he who seizes your infants
    and dashes them against the rocks.

It simply could not be happening. It was a
nightmare of apocalyptic proportions. Yet they

had seen it with their own eyes. They came like a swarm of giant locusts; murdering, looting, burning. Twice the beloved city of Jerusalem was laid siege. The second time was the worst – 589 BC. For eighteen months the poor beleaguered inhabitants of that city were reduced to skin and bone. Mothers ate their own offspring cooked over fires fuelled by human dung. It simply could not be happening, not to them of all people. After all, they were God's people – so they supposed – the apple of his eye, Moses had told them as much (Deut. 32:10). But here they were herded like cattle to occupy refugee camps strung like beads along the rivers of Babylon, the pagan nation which had all but annihilated them.

As they looked back over their journey of hundreds of miles, naturally they thought of Zion, God's holy hill and his holy city – and – they wept. It wasn't so much because the walls lay in ruins, the temple a charred remains – it was because of all that Jerusalem stood for which seemed to perish in the ashes. Jerusalem – the 'city of peace' – symbolising the peace of God, the presence of God, the prosperity of God, in short, all the promises of Yahweh were captured in that one word – Zion. Yes, how they wept.

But now they were exiles in a strange land, amongst a strange people, with strange customs and strange gods. That is when the taunts began. 'You Jews are renowned for your singing and dancing. Your religious festivities have been the talk of the nations – why don't you sing your songs now? After all you are "God's people",' they would say with a knowing smirk on their faces. But how could they sing the songs of Zion? Songs of hope and promise, when all hope is reduced to a pile of rubble? No, they would simply hang up their harps and weep.

Babylon now
That is the background to Psalm 137. But what may come as a surprise to many is the fact that Babylon still exists. Not the Babylon of King Nebuchadnezzar, now modern day Iraq. That perished long ago, seventy years or so after they had been crowing about their victory over the Jews. No, there is another Babylon which is to be understood as a human system set up in defiance against God. This is the way the Bible conceives 'Babylon' whose root meaning is possibly (and ironically) 'The gate of God' (Bab-ilim).

Genesis 10:8-12 traces back the idea of world domination to Babylon. In Genesis 11:1-9 the architecture of the giant temple of 'Babel', probably referring to Babylon's *ziggurat* E-tem-an-ki, is stigmatized as an expression of human pride that wishes to storm heaven itself. In Isaiah 14:1-23 Babylon seems to represent more than the historical empire of Nebuchadnezzar, it becomes a 'type' of the power which opens to evil men every possibility in the world, whose ruler tried to force his way into the assembly of the gods and fell.

This imagery of Babylon is taken up by the New Testament as a symbol of a human race in arrogant rebellion against the Lord and his people. The apostle Peter begins his first letter by addressing Christians as 'God's elect, *strangers* or, as the RSV translates it, *exiles* in the world, scattered' (1 Pet. 1:1) – just as these Jews were scattered. He ends by writing, 'She who is in *Babylon*, sends her greeting' (1 Pet. 5:13), a code for the church in the city of Rome, for then it was Rome which embodied the overweening pride which snubs God and defies his ways – Babylon. Nowhere is this more clearly seen than in the Book of Revelation where Babylon is mentioned time and time again as representing mankind in organised revolt against its Maker (Rev. 17–18).

The truth is: we live in Babylon.

As Western society moves further and further away from its Christian heritage, as we have been doing so very rapidly for the last sixty years or so, Christians will feel more and more like exiles living in Babylon. The question is: how can we sing the songs of the Lord in a strange land? That is, how can we live as God's people and witness to God's promises which are often captured in song when those around us either do not understand or simply do not want to know?

In his thoughtful reflections on what he calls the 'post-Christian mind', the writer and erstwhile pupil of C. S. Lewis, Harry Blamires, writing in 1999 argues:

There is no doubt that, as the twenty-first century approaches, Christendom faces formidable hostility, not least in those developed Western countries once regarded as bulwarks of Christian civilization. Looking around us, we Christians cannot but be aware of how powerful and insidious is the assault on the faith we hold, the faith we have assumed to be the foundation of Western culture. Current secularist humanism – a mishmash of relativistic notions negating traditional values and absolutes – infects the intellectual air we breathe. There is a campaign to undermine all human acknowledgement of the transcendent, to whittle away all human respect for objective restraints on the individualistic self. The hold of this campaign on the media is such that the masses are being brainwashed as they read the press, listen to the radio or watch TV.

Every area of life is being encroached upon by a new moral darkness: politics, education, law, medicine, the family – even the church. The philosopher Alisdair MacIntyre refers to 'new dark ages' of moral decay. Alexander Solzhenitsyn warns of the West's debilitating 'spiritual exhaustion'. In more recent years in a best-selling book, William Strauss and Neil Howe writing about the United States, maintain that 'it feels like it's unravelling'. The authors go on: 'Though we live in an era of relative peace and comfort, we have settled into a mood of pessimism about the long term future, fearful that our superpower nation is somehow rotting from within ... we perceive no greatness in our leaders, but a new meanness in ourselves. Small wonder that each new election brings a new jolt, its aftermath a new disappointment.' What can be said of the United States can also be said of Britain, because, as someone once remarked, America is the 'lead society', it usually gets there first but we get there in the end.

Think for a moment of the unravelling that has happened in our society during the last fifty years. Even a few decades ago, most people, even non-Christians, would have agreed that there were absolutes in morality – perhaps adhering to the golden rule or the Ten Commandments. That has largely disappeared as God has been side-lined to the edges of our society's thinking by the relentless process of secularisation. It is a truism that if we say goodbye to the Fatherhood of God it is only a matter of time before we say goodbye to the brotherhood of man. Or as C. S. Lewis remarked: 'We laugh at honour and are shocked to find traitors in our midst. We castrate and bid the geldings be fruitful.' If truth is rejected, moral decay follows in its wake.

The family has constantly been under attack. Fifty years ago the family was seen as the basic stable unit of society, and laws were in place to support that. Much of that has now gone with no-fault divorce and the promotion of alternative family life styles – including homosexual and lesbian ones.

Within the church, sixty years or so ago, William Temple delayed his consecration as Bishop because he had doubts about the historicity of the Virgin Birth and only when he came to a clear conclusion it was true did he go ahead. Now we have prominent church leaders who would question virtually anything miraculous – resurrection and all – and we no longer seem to be shocked.

Life too has been cheapened. Whatever the intentions of those who legislated for the 1967 Abortion Act, it would never have entered anyone's mind then that we would now find ourselves in a situation where a baby is being aborted at the rate of one every three minutes.

Think too of our children's behaviour. One Head Teacher related to me that one Local Education Authority considers a well-managed primary class one in which chairs are not being thrown across the room by pupils!

How far we have travelled in such a short space of time.

How 'wasms' have been changed by 'isms'

None of these things has happened by accident, they all flow from a significant change in the way people think and view the world. At the risk of oversimplification, let us consider just some of the 'isms' which have shaped the way our society is now thinking and so behaving. Christians must understand the Babylon in which they live if they are to seek to witness effectively and not simply be swept out with the tide.

First, there is *materialism*, that is the belief that reality only consists of that which can be seen and measured – there is no room for what might be called the transcendent. Such notions can be explained away in terms of psychology or sociology. Everything, it is argued, can be understood purely in terms of natural causes, there is no room for God. If there is an overarching 'metanarrative' which holds our view of the world together, it is that we are all products of blind, meaningless chance. Not surprisingly in the preface to Stephen Hawking's best seller *A Brief History of Time* the atheist astronomer Carl Sagan writes:

> The word God fills these pages. Hawking embarks on a quest to answer Einstein's famous question about whether God had any choice in creating a universe. Hawking is attempting, as he explicitly states, to understand the mind of God. And this makes all the more unexpected the conclusion of

the effort, at least so far: a universe with no edge in time, no beginning or end in time, and nothing for a Creator to do.

In other words, who needs God? – this scientific description rules him out.

But there is a price to pay when everything is reduced to chance. Humans can't have any significance or meaning and all we can live for is the now. Imagine some spilt milk on the kitchen floor. It is there by accident. Does it have any meaning? Suppose that by some freak of nature that spilt milk gains consciousness. Just by declaring itself to have significance, does such a declaration give it any more significance than it had before? Of course not – an accident is simply that – an accident. But that is what we are left with because of the Evolutionism taught in our schools and colleges – *we* are nothing but accidents. And so it will not be long before people start treating each other like accidents, as indeed, we have already seen with children in the United States walking into school with guns to blow their classmates away. We may be shocked but we should not be surprised. Eventually people will start living out what they have been taught.

Secondly, there is *individualism*. In 1979 the sociologist Robert Bellah conducted a survey of two hundred average middle-class Americans and published his findings in a book called *Habits of the Heart*. His conclusion?: 'many had no sense of community or social obligation. They saw the world as a fragmented place for choice and freedom that produced little meaning and comfort.' In short 'I' rules. The focus is on me, my comforts, my pleasures, my choices.

Much of this goes back to the eighteenth-century French thinker Jean Jacques Rousseau who believed that man was naturally good and all that was necessary was for people to be set free from the restraints of society and the church. The anti-authority mood of the swinging sixties captured this for many, spawning the demanding inflationary outlook of the 1970s, the 'loadsa money' generation of Thatcher's eighties and now the rave culture of Blair's 2,001. Hence, the emphasis on *individual* choice. To an earlier generation it mattered *what* we chose – do the right thing; now all that matters is *that* we choose – I must decide, for that alone gives me a sense of value. The bitter irony is that for all the increase in talk about freedom we seem to be less and less free as a society. How many of those who are now over forty, when they were children, used to walk several miles to school alone, or played in the woods unsupervised? How many of us would allow such freedom to our children now? We do not. That freedom has pretty well evaporated because people have been allowed to be 'free' to follow their own desires especially in the realm of sex and violence with the result that young men, let alone women and children, do not feel safe to walk the streets at night.

Thirdly, there is *hedonism*, the pursuit of pleasure via the route of *subjectivism,* that is, what is real is what I feel. If this world is all there is, then it is for this world I must live and live it now. I won't get a second chance when I die, that is the end. And who cares about future generations? – they don't exist, so why should I feel obliged to them? Consequently I can build up a debt with impunity and any 'future' generation which happens to come along can pick up the tab.

Many people may not know what they think, but they know what they feel and how they want to feel – which is to feel good. The recent Vodka ad on the billboards of England said it all. With pictures of trendy young people celebrating the dawn with drinks in hand, emblazoned in bold type were the words 'Sleep when you're dead'. In other words, there will be plenty of time to sleep after you die, now is the time to party. That is why no government is going to be able to deal with the increasing drug problem. How can they when it is the generation which now forms the ruling classes which has peddled the idea that pleasure, rather than principles, rules. If drugs do it for you, who is to say it is wrong?

Which brings us to the final 'ism', *relativism*. That is, what is true is what is true for me. There are no absolute truths, right or wrong, good or bad – so don't judge, it's all relative to your culture or your upbringing. The classic showcase for this is the Jerry Springer show in which any perversion can be displayed: a daughter-in-law who is now having a sexual relationship with her mother-in-law to the utter distress of the husband who has just found out in front of millions of viewers, but is told, 'Why not, they love each other? Who are you to impose your morality on them?'

Perceptively, Harry Blamires describes the process whereby such a relativistic mindset undermines the traditional understanding of the family:

The process of destroying standards relies heavily on the tendentious use of words. We do not find many people openly declaring war on 'the family'. The method of attack is to keep and use the word 'family' but destroy its meaning. By this means the standards which usage of the word has previously sustained are obliterated. That is why the enemy of the true family does not usually condemn 'the family' in so many words. Instead new terms are brought into use. We hear criticism of the 'nuclear family' or the 'traditional family'. The propaganda advantage in popularising such expressions is obvious. 'Family' is a word which, over the centuries, has acquired warm, humane associations. Idealized pictures of conventional family groupings survive in art, in literature and in popular memory. The word 'family' is likely to arouse emotive associations of homeliness, affection and warmth. The technique is to take over the traditional concept and deny its traditional exclusiveness – the thing that makes it what it is. Instead of attacking the 'family' as such, they turn what we have always known as the 'family' into a variant amongst other variants. In fact, the non-family (the very thing that the concept of the 'family' exists to exclude) becomes a 'family' too – perhaps two lesbians who are bringing up a child conceived in a test tube. Once the verbal process starts – of qualifying the norm of speaking of the 'traditional' or 'two-parent' family – the game is lost. The assumption has been accepted that there are other kinds of families too.

This is Babylon, with its strange language where words can mean whatever you want them to mean, where right and wrong have been excluded, where the gods of pleasure and self reign supreme, and where everything is relative therefore religion must be kept private. These are the ideas which have been disseminated with remarkable effect through the media. Whether it is a highbrow programme like *Question Time* or more lowbrow like *Eastenders*, these are the views which are being put across and in which our minds are marinating. It is therefore now possible to have a whole evening on Channel 4 called 'Gaynight' – it is an alternative. Can we imagine a whole evening called 'Christian night'? It was Groucho Marx who quipped, 'I find television very educating. Every time somebody turns on the set

I go into the other room and read a book.' He may have had a point.

On being counter cultural
Let us return to the question of verse 4 in Psalm 137: 'How can we sing the songs of the LORD while in a foreign land?'

Two principles.

Negatively, don't compromise. What is the call by the pagans to God's people to sing anything else but a call to 'settle down'? The taunt is implicit in the demand to sing in verse 3: 'Why not recognise that this is your home for good? There is no point in moping: simply come to terms with your situation. Join us and sing.' An earlier Christian generation had a word for it – they called it 'worldliness'. Sadly, many in the church have succumbed to just that, often without realising it. They have set the Lord's songs to a different tune, that of the world, Christianising what are essentially alien beliefs and practices.

Consequently, we have the 'Christian materialist' which paradoxically manifests himself in two ways.

First, those who deny the miraculous, like the former Bishop of Durham, David Jenkins, dismissing the resurrection of Jesus as a 'conjuring trick with bones'. This is a position which is essentially modernist, a product of the so-called Enlightenment which *a priori* rules out the miraculous; everything must be explained in purely naturalistic terms of cause and effect.

On the other hand there are those who see God *only* in what is called the 'supernatural', the weird and the strange. They do not seem to recognize his hand at all in the ordinary – the rise of the sun, the dance of the atoms, or the birth of a baby. Or if it is recognised it is somehow inferior to the alleged 'signs and wonders' on show. Whereas the former position rules God out from working in his universe, this position restricts God's work to the inexplicable. This brand of Christianity, which the late Francis Schaeffer termed 'the new super-spirituality', is demand-driven with the result that everything has to be entertaining thrills which leads to church services taking on the appearance of a circus. In effect there has been a surrender to the materialistic mindset and God has been effectively reduced to a 'god of the gaps' or to be more precise 'a god of the strange'.

There is also the 'Christian hedonism'. Here Christianity is portrayed as one long party, full of ups, no downs. The main thing is the 'feel good factor'. Talk of taking up a cross is a switch off, devoid of selling power and so must be abandoned.

Then we have the 'Christian relativist'. The church at which I was a curate is, as I write, in the midst of an unholy row because the Vicar, quite rightly, considers it inappropriate for the choir master to remain in post given that he is living with a woman and not married to her. But relativism has reared its head in the congregation: 'Who is the Vicar to say what is right or wrong? As long as they are sincere what does it matter?'

Of course, it is tempting to sing to the tune of the world, for if you don't, persecution is just around the corner, as Daniel and his friends found to their own cost in Babylon – and, so shall we.

More positively we can challenge by singing as loudly as possible the *Lord's* song, which for Christians is the gospel – the word of Christ according to Colossians 3:16: 'Let the word of Christ dwell in you [plural] richly as you teach and admonish each other will all wisdom, and as you sing psalms, hymns and spiritual songs, with gratitude in your hearts to God.' We might well legitimately construe such 'singing' as a metaphor for gospel proclamation (which is certainly Paul's burden in Colossians 1:28: 'We proclaim him, admonishing and teaching everyone with all wisdom, so that we might present everyone perfect in Christ').

At least the people depicted in the Psalm had the right priorities: 'If I forget you, O Jerusalem, may my right hand forget its skill. May my tongue cling to the roof of my mouth if I do not consider... Jerusalem my highest joy' (v.5). Having been put into exile as punishment for their sin, the people were at last waking up to the fact that God and his covenant came first, as symbolised by Jerusalem.

But where they made the mistake was in thinking that God was so tightly wedded to the symbol he was restricted – he was back home and they were in Babylon. In stark contrast the message of Ezekiel, who was one of the captives, was that God was *with* his people in Babylon (Ezek. 1). The temple may have been destroyed, but not God. Neither his power nor purposes had diminished.

It is this same divine power and purpose which find their fulfilment in Jesus who came to deliver God's people from a spiritual exile far worse than that experienced by the Jews. (Note for instance how Matthew's genealogy, divided into three fourteen generations, sees the exile as a major turning point in salvation-history pointing to the coming of Jesus: 'Thus there were fourteen generations in all from Abraham to David, fourteen from David to the *exile* to Babylon, and fourteen from the *exile* to the Christ' [Matt. 1:17]). Christians not only can but must sing the Lord's song in this strange land because of what God has achieved in his Son Jesus.

Was it not the risen Jesus who in sending his disciples out into a hostile world said, 'I will be with you always' (Matt. 28:20)? Are Christians not the new temple being built in 'Babylon' with Christ dwelling in their midst by his Spirit (1 Cor. 3:16)? We can sing because God is present. And as we sing, God proclaims, for when we 'sing' the Lord's song by word and deed, we declare

God's truth and so challenge an unbelieving world which lives a lie – the lie that this life is all there is, that I am number one and that personal pleasure is to be pursued at all costs.

What is more, this 'song' is also a song of judgment: 'Remember, O LORD, what the Edomites did on the day Jerusalem fell. "Tear it down," they cried, "tear it down to its foundations!" O Daughter of Babylon, doomed to destruction, happy is he who repays you for what you have done to us – he who seizes your infants and dashes them against the rocks' (v. 7). The Psalmist may have used language which hurts our sensitive ears, but he strains towards an important truth, namely, that the Judge of the earth will do what is right. Christians can say from one viewpoint he already has. For the God of truth came into this world in the person of Jesus to save this world from its headlong dash towards Hell and its precursor – that new darkness we are now busily pursuing as we dismantle civilization and call it postmodernity. He bore our guilt on his shoulders, showing he is a just God (Rom. 3:26). He destroyed death and in so doing declared this life is not the be all and end all, calling us to discover true pleasure, a soul which finds its delight in serving him and each other. But one day the Judge will return and we shall be called to give an account (Acts 17:31). No one will be able to hide then behind the claim that truth is simply a social construct. Because for God truth is not relative – it is absolute. Right and wrong still exist, his character is their measure, and people rather than possessions matter eternally. Furthermore, it is as God's people start to *live* as people of light, showing there is another way, a better way, singing the *Lord's* song in all its fullness, that the darkness can begin to turn to dawn.

Chapter 2

Sez Who?

Romans 1:16-32

[16]I am not ashamed of the gospel, because it is the power of God for the salvation of everyone who believes: first for the Jew, then for the Gentile. [17]For in the gospel a righteousness from God is revealed, a righteousness that is by faith from first to last, just as it is written: 'The righteous will live by faith.'

[18]The wrath of God is being revealed from heaven against all the godlessness and wickedness of men who suppress the truth by their wickedness, [19]since what may be known about God is plain to them, because God has made it plain to them. [20]For since the creation of the world God's invisible qualities – his eternal power and divine nature – have been clearly seen, being understood from what has been made, so that men are without excuse.

[21]For although they knew God, they neither glorified him as God nor gave thanks to him, but their thinking became futile and their foolish hearts were darkened. [22]Although they claimed to be wise, they became fools [23]and exchanged the glory of the immortal God for images made to look like mortal man and birds and animals and reptiles.

[24]Therefore God gave them over in the sinful desires of their hearts to sexual impurity for the degrading of their bodies with one another. [25]They exchanged the truth of God for a lie, and worshipped and served created things rather than the Creator – who is forever praised. Amen.

[26]Because of this, God gave them over to shameful lusts. Even their women exchanged natural relations for unnatural ones. [27]In the same way the men also

abandoned natural relations with women and were inflamed with lust for one another. Men committed indecent acts with other men, and received in themselves the due penalty for their perversion.

[28]Furthermore, since they did not think it worthwhile to retain the knowledge of God, he gave them over to a depraved mind, to do what ought not to be done. [29]They have become filled with every kind of wickedness, evil, greed and depravity. They are full of envy, murder, strife, deceit and malice. They are gossips, [30]slanderers, God-haters, insolent, arrogant and boastful; they invent ways of doing evil; they disobey their parents; [31]they are senseless, faithless, heartless, ruthless. [32]Although they know God's righteous decree that those who do such things deserve death, they not only continue to do these very things but also approve of those who practice them.

He was identified as 'Patient Zero' – the initial carrier of the AIDS HIV virus in the United States. His name was Gaetan Dugas, a French Canadian airline steward. Before his death in 1984, Dugas estimated that he had had sexual liaisons with 2,500 partners in New York and Californian bathhouses, rest rooms, bars and motels. Even after he had been told by doctors that he had this fatal sexually-transmitted disease, he continued to infect dozens of partners. 'I've got gay cancer,' he would tell them afterwards, perversely enjoying the merging of sex and death.

We may be tempted to dismiss Dugas simply as mentally deranged, one of those unfortunate sociopaths that life occasionally throws up. But let's pause and think of another possible way of looking at the situation.

If all morality is relative – so that what is good for you isn't necessarily good for me, and it is directed only by the goal of gaining maximum personal happiness – then why not do what he did? If there is no absolute right and wrong, and we are merely the products of blind meaningless chance, coming from nowhere and going nowhere, then who is to say what is good or bad? Society perhaps? But, what is society but a collection of individuals who will eventually die, so why should I put the alleged well-being of society above my own well-being in terms of personal pleasure and fulfilment? We come up against what the Yale Law Professor, Arthur Leff, has termed 'the grand Sez who?' He argues that if there is no God, no transcendent source of value, then there is no universally accepted source of authority. We object to Serbs that genocide is wrong. 'Sez who? You wouldn't object to killing a thousand ants would you, so why not a thousand people?' We tell our youngsters that vandalism is objectionable. 'Sez who? Those who have property and are well off anyway and can buy their fun? It's every man and woman for himself.' You may object, 'But I don't believe in God and yet I don't do these things.' That may well be true, but there is no compelling *reason* to offer to anyone else why they shouldn't, except they might get caught, and in the long term they will be unhappy if society descends into chaos, so we will all be losers. But that still doesn't provide us with a *moral* reason why not.

What's the problem?

A few years ago, Professor Christie Davies of Reading University carried out a study called 'Moralisation and Demoralisation' and charted the rise in crime and social disorder in Britain over the last 150 years. He showed that while housing conditions and poverty were far worse at the beginning of the twentieth century than at the end, the reported incidence of serious crime was far less. He comments on the situation today in these terms: 'For the Left the villain is capitalism and for the Right it is welfare; both are ways of avoiding the conclusion that wicked and irresponsible choices are made by wicked and irresponsible individuals.' In other words, the problem at root is a moral one.

Little wonder that we find ourselves in the midst of a moral crisis as diseased ideas are so easily spread by the 'New Class' through the media.

In his book *The Abolition of Britain*, the journalist Peter Hitchens helpfully gives several examples of this 'immorality dissemination' taking place through the popular 'soaps' which tend to attract the largest TV audiences: '*Brookside* upset many early viewers in its early days because the characters used too much bad language. Phil Redmond immediately toned it down. Yet the same programme has featured mercy-killing by suffocation, lesbian kissing and incest between brother and sister. As Anna Pukas wrote in the *Daily Express* in 1997: 'In *Eastenders* and *Brookside*, the taboos fell thick and fast. Drug addiction, male and female homosexuality, incest, child abuse – sometimes it seemed as though the writers had been told to churn out scripts on Perversion of the Month.' This 'dumbing down' has been extended to the longer established soaps too, such as *Coronation Street*.

Hitchens continues: 'In *Coronation Street*, residents were made to undergo the arrival in their midst of a male-to-female transsexual, who was denied access to the ladies' loo at work by cruel prejudice. By a strange paradox, this person was played by a female actor, subtly suggesting that a switch from one sex to the other really is possible. The story-line was immediately praised by a Labour MP, who suggested it would help win full civil rights for transsexuals, full civil rights meaning the ability to alter the facts on their birth certificates.'

He then shrewdly adds: 'The pattern in all these events is the same. Behaviour which was once deviant is made to seem mainstream, or at least acceptable, and those who are unhappy about it are portrayed as narrow-minded, old-fashioned, prejudiced and wrong. The effect of this implicit propaganda upon public opinion has been enormous, causing many people to be ashamed of views they had held since their childhood and had thought until recently were normal.'

There is a deep moral problem in our society, a moral decay which extends to the very foundations.

The Bible, however, would go even further and say that at root the problem is a spiritual one, and it is to the spiritual diagnosis of the apostle Paul that we turn in Romans 1:18ff.

The problem of judgement

Here Paul is describing his own world, but notice how remarkably similar it is to ours. He is painting in dark hues, a world in a state of moral decay – indeed, any society which turns its back on its Maker and his laws – for the result is always the same, an initial gradual declension and eventually a rapid social slide into chaos. When Rome eventually fell to the Barbarian hordes, it was not because the opposing armies were militarily superior, it was because the Roman Empire had become so morally flabby and internally weak, they were a pushover, with no will to fight, with nothing to defend, save personal pleasure, and certainly no principle. They were not the first civilization to go that way and neither will they be the last.

When you think about it, what Paul describes in these pages, and what we see unfolding around us, is nothing but a re-enactment of the original sin of Adam with its attendant miseries as recorded in Genesis 1–3. Paul refers to the creation of the world (v. 20), the classification of the creatures into birds, mammals and reptiles (v. 23); he uses terms of Genesis in speaking of 'glory', 'image' and 'likeness'. Paul alludes to humanity's knowledge of God (vv. 19, 21), its desire to become 'wise' (v. 22), as well as its refusal to remain a creature dependent on its Maker (vv. 18, 21); instead it foolishly is willing to exchange God's truth for the lie of Satan (v. 25), a rebellion deserving death (v. 32). In other words, the various manifestations of the falling apart of our world are all signs of a world on the run from God. What Adam did, we still do, because we have inherited his nature in wanting to mount a royal coup and oust God from his rightful place on the throne of the universe and put ourselves there – like the King of Babylon in fact (cf. Isaiah 14). To a lesser or greater degree we all do it. But the fallout becomes worse when society institutionalises the rebellion, when good is called bad and bad is called good because there is no reason for thinking otherwise.

But Paul's spiritual analysis goes even further than that. For not only is ours a world on the run from God, it is a world under the judgment of God:

> The wrath of God is being revealed from heaven against all the godlessness and wickedness of men who suppress the truth by their wickedness (v.18).

This is God's measured and righteous judicial response to our arrogant and wilful declaration of UDI. We willingly take the Maker's gifts but we refuse to show him either the glory or gratitude. 'For although they knew God, they neither glorified him as God nor gave thanks to him' (v. 21a).

So why the wrath? Paul tells us in verses 18-23.

I am sure that you have noticed that very small children think that if they cover their eyes they really do believe you are not there, they think they are able to make you disappear. Paul says that is precisely what we all tend to do with God (vv. 19-20):

> since what may be known about God is plain to them, because God has made it plain to them. For since the creation of the world God's invisible qualities – his eternal power and divine nature – have been clearly seen, being understood from what has been made, so that men are without excuse.

When you go to an art gallery and view some of the paintings there, you don't think for a moment that those works of art came into being all by themselves. As you look at a painting, part of your mind will go to the artist himself, maybe thinking what an incredible imagination he has, what skill he displays in transferring those thoughts via brush strokes and pigments on to canvas. Similarly, God has taken steps to make himself known through what he has made. God in himself is invisible and eternal, but through what can be seen in space and time he communicates to us something of his divine nature, his divine artistry if you like. What is more, there is within each one of us, according to verse 21, a knowledge of God, perhaps more of a *sense* of God – that awareness deep down that there is someone who has made us and for whom we were made; we are creatures of a Creator. That much we *do* know.

But what do we do with that knowledge? Use it to seek after him all the more? Not according to Paul and not according to experience – verse 18: we '*suppress* the truth by [our] wickedness', our 'thinking' (v. 21a) 'becomes futile and our foolish hearts darkened. Claiming to be wise we become fools, exchanging the glory of the immortal God for images made to look like mortal men and animals' (vv. 21-23).

Whatever becomes the centre of our lives, our thinking, our drive for living, that is our idol – our substitute god. We are by nature worshipping creatures. Our rebellion shows itself in shifting our focus of attention from the Creator to the creature: 'They exchanged the truth of God for a lie, and worshipped and served created things rather than the Creator – who is forever praised. Amen' (v. 25).

It is important to notice the process by which this spiritual and moral decline takes place. We are often fed the view that the great thinkers, who have shaped the modern world in its rejection of Christianity and the Christian heritage, have done so as a result of detached intellectual wrestling. So that as a matter of intellectual integrity, the old order had to be overthrown. Nothing could be further from the truth. The key phrase is in verse 24: the 'sinful *desires* of their hearts'.

In his book *Intellectuals*, Paul Johnson has shown that whether it is Rousseau and his concern for individual freedom or Karl Marx and his alleged concern for the workers, deep down they were driven by what can only be described as egocentric desires. The impulses came first and some form of justification of their ideas came second. He concludes:

> The belief seems to be spreading that intellectuals are no wiser as mentors, or worthier as exemplars, than the witch doctors or priests of old. I share that scepticism. A dozen people picked at random on the street are at heart as likely to offer sensible views on moral and political matters as a

cross-section of the intelligentsia. But I would go further. One of the principle lessons of our tragic [twentieth] century, which has seen so many millions of innocent lives sacrificed to improve the lot of humanity, is – beware intellectuals.

Let us take one example of someone who has changed the West's outlook on sex and especially homosexuality, perhaps more than any other, the American zoologist Alfred Kinsey. In 1948 and 1953 he produced two very influential reports which, amongst other things, claimed that 10% of the male population were predominately homosexual.

Did Kinsey pursue his studies with scientific detachment with no axe to grind? Not according to his biographer James H. Jones. Kinsey himself was both homosexual and a sado-masochist who encouraged his research team to have sex with each other and his wife, which he filmed in their attic. He also fixed his research results to support his lifestyle. Far from taking representative samples from the male population at large to determine sexual orientation and practice, 26% of his subjects were sex offenders and a further 25% were in prison, the rest were male prostitutes and pimps. Worse still, is the more recent evidence that he employed and trained paedophiles. Don't forget, this work provided much of the basis for the loosening of society's attitudes towards sexual activity from the 1960s to the present day. Do you see what was driving this scientific research? Certainly not the pursuit of objective truth but sadly his own lusts, sex which had become his idol.

Os Guinness in *Time for Truth*, an important treatment of postmodernity, poses the choice we all face: 'Either we conform the truth to our desires or we conform our desires to the truth.' He goes on to write:

> Stated baldly in this challenge, the Jewish and Christian view of truth flies directly in the face of modern views, just as ... with postmodern views. Expressed most powerfully in the Enlightenment, the modern view of truth made two claims: first, that truth is objective, certain and knowable by the unaided intellect without the interference of personal distortions; and second, that the freer the thinker, the more he or she is committed to the fearless pursuit of truth at any cost. The biblical position rejects both these claims as pretentious and false. As human beings we are by nature truth-seekers; as fallen human beings we are also by nature truth-twisters. And a proper account of truth in the human project must do justice to both.

That account we see in Paul's treatment in the book of Romans. It is in their *wickedness* that men suppress the truth, extolling what is perverse to be natural and claiming to be intellectually sophisticated and wise in the process. Turn your back on God and you do not embrace agnosticism, you embrace a lie. How can God ignore that and be true to himself? How can anyone with an ounce of moral sense in their being simply shrug their shoulders and say 'so what?' Such a state of affairs demands a reaction-justice, *God's* justice.

The signs of judgement

Note in verse 18 that the present tense is used: 'The wrath of God is *being* revealed.' It is something taking place now. How it is being shown is revealed in that telling phrase which is repeated three times, 'God gave them over': 'he gave them over in their sinful desires' (v. 24); 'God gave them over to shameful lust' (v. 26); 'God gave them over to a depraved mind' (v. 28). In other words, the perversion *is* the punishment. This is what people want and so this is what people will get. God allows us to go our own way and suffer the consequences, personal and social, as we are sadly seeing today. But this is not simply retributive punishment, being given over to the prison of our own desires – the permissiveness which we foolishly mistake for freedom – it is in some measure restorative, the hope being that people will eventually recognise the folly and the destructive nature of living without God and his laws and so will eventually turn to him for rescue. In fact this is the direction of Paul's argument up to chapter three, demonstrating that we are all in the same needy boat and there is only one solution – Christ and the Cross.

The solution to judgement

'I am not ashamed of the gospel, because it is the power of God for the salvation of everyone who believes: first for the Jew, then for the Gentile. For in the gospel a righteousness from God is revealed, a righteousness that is by faith from first to last, just as it is written: "The righteous will live by faith"' (vv. 16-17). Our laws and many of our public institutions did not come from nowhere; they have grown over many years out of the rich deep soil of the Christian faith – the belief that there is a God who is truth, who has spoken in the Bible, who has given us a conscience which accuses us when we go against the grain of the moral order of the universe. It tells of a Creator who has made men and women in his image. They are so precious in his sight that he sent his one and only Son to the cross to show his righteousness in punishing our sin as he took our place. Because of the work of Christ, God restores us back to himself as his children. We are forgiven and empowered by the Holy Spirit when we put our trust in him. This is the gospel of which Paul speaks. 'Gospel' – the good news – is the answer to the bad news of which we have been thinking and which is in evidence all around us, a world under the judgement of God. It is God's way of making bad people into his good friends. What is more, when this happens, society is changed and enriched. History proves this time and time again.

Not for the first time has Britain found herself in Romans chapter 1. We may think things are bad now, but there was a time when they were perhaps even worse.

In 1684, 527,000 gallons of spirits were distilled in England. By 1750 the consumption of spirits had risen to 11,000,000 gallons. Gin was the drug problem of the day. MPs were often too drunk to carry out parliamentary business in the afternoon. A favourite saying at the time was, 'To be as drunk as a lord', meaning a 'Lord Bishop' – the Church was that bad. Gambling was a national obsession, with personal debt crippling many. Then there was the treatment of children. Many parish churches set up special institutions to 'care' for orphans, especially the unwanted offspring of prostitutes, which was an epidemic. It appears so kind, doesn't it? That is until you consider the contemporary surveys carried out which showed that the vast majority placed into such care died by the age of twelve months. Some were deliberately murdered and thrown onto the local rubbish tip. Some of the men and women running these places decided to send children out to beg, and to ensure greater pity, and so more cash, forcibly maimed them, amputating a limb or blinding an eye. This was a time, at the beginning of the eighteenth century, when it was being taught that if there is a God at all he is remote and uninterested, that reason is the answer to all our problems and the satisfaction of the senses paramount. This was Britain – the moral leper of Europe.

Then in 1735 God raised up a twenty-year-old Church of England curate called George Whitefield, and later the Wesley brothers and others like Howell Harris, who preached this message of Romans to the masses. The result? The country was set ablaze in Christian revival. It was a time when thousands from every stratum of society came to know the living Christ for themselves and had their lives turned around. The spiritual descendants of these men were people like Wilberforce and Shaftesbury who went on to bring about the great social changes we enjoy today. But it was the gospel which was the driving force, shaping a nation.

Isn't that what we desperately need today? For our hearts to be set alight by God's Spirit through the gospel? The need for churches to become communities of light? For each one of us who calls Jesus Christ Lord, to be seeking ways of demonstrating his kingdom? For there to be Christian schools which show there is a better way – the only way – and that is to get back in touch with Reality, the One who has clearly given us his commands and principles, but more than that, his Spirit of moral power when we humbly turn to His Son? There is only One to whom we can turn for mercy.

Chapter 3

Living Amongst the Idols

Isaiah 44:6-23

[6]'This is what the LORD says –
   Israel's King and Redeemer, the LORD Almighty:
I am the first and I am the last;
   apart from me there is no God.
[7]Who then is like me? Let him proclaim it.
   Let him declare and lay out before me
what has happened since I established my ancient
   people,
   and what is yet to come –
   yes, let him foretell what will come.
[8]Do not tremble, do not be afraid.
   Did I not proclaim this and foretell it long ago?
You are my witnesses. Is there any God besides me?
   No, there is no other Rock; I know not one.'

[9]All who make idols are nothing,
   and the things they treasure are worthless.
Those who would speak up for them are blind;
   they are ignorant, to their own shame.
[10]Who shapes a god and casts an idol,
   which can profit him nothing?
[11]He and his kind will be put to shame;
   craftsmen are nothing but men.
Let them all come together and take their stand;
   they will be brought down to terror and infamy.

[12]The blacksmith takes a tool
   and works with it in the coals;
he shapes an idol with hammers,
   he forges it with the might of his arm.
He gets hungry and loses his strength;

he drinks no water and grows faint.
¹³The carpenter measures with a line
and makes an outline with a marker;
he roughs it out with chisels
and marks it with compasses.
He shapes it in the form of man,
of man in all his glory,
that it may dwell in a shrine.
¹⁴He cut down cedars,
or perhaps took a cypress or oak.
He let it grow among the trees of the forest,
or planted a pine, and the rain made it grow.
¹⁵It is man's fuel for burning;
some of it he takes and warms himself,
he kindles a fire and bakes bread.
But he also fashions a god and worships it;
he makes an idol and bows down to it.
¹⁶Half of the wood he burns in the fire;
over it he prepares his meal,
he roasts his meat and eats his fill.
He also warms himself and says,
'Ah! I am warm; I see the fire.'
¹⁷From the rest he makes a god, his idol;
he bows down to it and worships.
He prays to it and says,
'Save me; you are my god.'
¹⁸They know nothing, they understand nothing;
their eyes are plastered over so that they cannot
see,
and their minds closed so that they cannot
understand.
¹⁹No-one stops to think,
no-one has the knowledge or understanding to say,

'Half of it I used for fuel;
  I even baked bread over its coals,
  I roasted meat and I ate.
Shall I make a detestable thing from what is left?
  Shall I bow down to a block of wood?'
²⁰He feeds on ashes, a deluded heart misleads him;
  he cannot save himself, or say,
  'Is not this thing in my right hand a lie?'

²¹'Remember these things, O Jacob,
  for you are my servant, O Israel.
I have made you, you are my servant;
  O Israel, I will not forget you.
²²I have swept away your offences like a cloud,
  your sins like the morning mist.
Return to me,
  for I have redeemed you.'

²³Sing for joy, O heavens, for the LORD has done this;
  shout aloud, O earth beneath.
Burst into song, you mountains,
  you forests and all your trees,
for the LORD has redeemed Jacob,
  he displays his glory in Israel.

Did you know that eight out of ten cats prefer *Whiskas*? That every third child born into the world is Chinese? Some people are fascinated with statistics. Of course, sometimes the statistics can be misinterpreted as with the case of the man from Dublin who, upon hearing that by using a certain gas heater he could cut his heating bills by half, decided that by having two of them he would never have to pay another heating bill in his life! But not only can statistics be misinterpreted – they can be misleading. We are told that over 75% of the population of Britain believes in God. But what does that mean? Just think of the word 'believe' for a moment. What would that involve for a Christian? At least three things. First, the Christian *worships* the God who has revealed himself in Jesus Christ. This is more than singing hymns and saying prayers, it is a matter of what you give your heart to as the centre of your world. Secondly, he or she *serves* God, which is more than professing allegiance, it is about what your ultimate ends in life are in the way you occupy yourself. But thirdly, belief involves *proclamation* or, if you like, advertising what you believe by what you say and do. So with this idea of belief in mind, when Joe Bloggs says 'I believe in God' and his main thought and overall direction in life is to climb up the ladder of promotion and maximise personal pleasure which includes promiscuous sex, surely it is a lie. But supposing the answer we get from Bill Bates is, 'No I don't believe in God,' and yet what he passionately believes in is making money, racing cars and gambling on the horses. He too is lying, because he believes in several gods – money, cars and horses. In fact there is no real difference between Joe and Bill. So the question which our pollsters should be asking is not 'Do you believe in God?' but 'Which *gods* do you believe in?' The Bible calls this idolatry. We are a nation full of idols and they are tearing us apart. God's people today are in 'Babylon' which is just as powerful and alluring as the literal Babylon in which the Jews found themselves in Exile. If Christians are going to learn how to deal with the surrounding idolatries they could do no better than to turn to Isaiah 44 and its monumental attack on the idols of those times.

The reality of idolatry

There certainly was nothing unreal about idolatry for these Jews when this prophecy came to them afresh as they were exiled in Babylon – the place was packed with them. Not only were there the ornate wooden statues of their gods – Bel, Nebo, Marduk (46:1) – but the great city of Babylon was one huge idol – a glorious self-tribute to the power and might of the greatest Empire the world had ever known. Of course the temptation for the Jews was to accommodate, to integrate these new gods into their religion, which was one reason why they were in exile in the first place. From the golden calf onward they simply couldn't resist having love affairs with idolatry and God had to teach them a painful lesson. So God, as it were, rubs their noses in it – verses 12-13:

¹²The blacksmith takes a tool
    and works with it in the coals;
he shapes an idol with hammers,
    he forges it with the might of his arm.
He gets hungry and loses his strength;
    he drinks no water and grows faint.
¹³The carpenter measures with a line
    and makes an outline with a marker;
he roughs it out with chisels
    and marks it with compasses.

This is going on all around them and it is enough to make their stomachs turn.

The temptation to idolatry is just as real for us living this side of the New Testament as it was for the Jews their side of the Old Testament. The apostle Paul broadens the prohibition on idols to include greed and immorality: 'For of this you can be sure: No immoral, impure or greedy person – such a man is an idolater – has any inheritance in the kingdom of Christ and of God' (Eph. 5:5) and 'Put to death, therefore, whatever belongs to your earthly nature: sexual immorality, impurity, lust, evil desires and greed, which is idolatry' (Col. 3:5). The very last words of the apostle John in his first letter are: 'Dear children, keep yourselves free from idols' (1 John 5:21). He certainly wouldn't have said that if it were not a real threat.

Idolatry isn't just a matter of making statues and bowing down to them, it is a matter of having faith in the wrong things, putting other things where God alone should be. The writer Harry Blamires describes it like this:

> We live in what is, in effect, a polytheistic society in what we give ourselves, with varying degrees of what can only be called idolatry, to the service of money making, career making, power grabbing, food, drink, fashion, entertainment, cars, gambling, sex and so on. This assertion does not imply that no man can give attention to these things without guilt. There is a due degree of attention that such things merit. But in fact they are getting excessive attention. As objects of concern they are attracting the kind and degree of human response more proper to the religious sphere. They have become objects of devotion.

Whatever we think is worth living for, worth sacrificing for, worth advertising to others – that is our idol.

What is more, ideas can become idols as they are transformed into ideologies. We not only make metal images but mental images. Speaking of the revival of fascism in parts of Europe, Charles Colson writes:

> The academic world is reeling from the discovery that two of the most influential scholars of modern times – Martin Heidegger and Paul de Man – were once Nazis. But perhaps it should not really be surprising that fascism is re-emerging. Human beings are incurably religious. The Russian novelist Fyodor Dostoyevsky once wrote that a person

'cannot live without worshipping something'. Anyone who rejects the true God must worship an idol. An idol is not necessarily a figure of wood or stone. It can also be an idea or set of ideas put forth to explain the world without God. An ideology.

All idolatry involves some form of infatuation. In verse 9 we see the infatuation of the emotions: 'All who make idols are nothing and the things *they treasure* are worthless.' They are things they 'treasure' or delight in. Someone has translated it as their 'little darlings' – the things they get excited about. In verses 18-20 it is the infatuation of the mind which is the target of Isaiah's taunt, people think such idols are full of knowledge and understanding, the sure road to enlightenment:

[18]They know nothing, they understand nothing;
 their eyes are plastered over so that they cannot see,
 and their minds closed so that they cannot understand.
[19]No one stops to think,
 no one has the knowledge or understanding to say,

 'Half of it I used for fuel;
 I even baked bread over its coals,
 I roasted meat and I ate.
Shall I make a detestable thing from what is left?
 Shall I bow down to a block of wood?'
[20]He feeds on ashes, a deluded heart misleads him;
 he cannot save himself, or say,
 'Is not this thing in my right hand a lie?'

They are, of course, nothing of the sort, they are a sign of dim thinking, for how can that which one moment is used to light an oven to bake bread be venerated the next moment as a god? It is plain stupid.

So we too have our idols which excite the emotions and capture the imagination, all a function of a world on the run from its Maker – Babylon. We may not have our temples devoted to Marduk but nonetheless we have our temples devoted to Mammon. The churches may be empty but the DIY stores are full. Cathedrals may be falling down but multiplex cinemas are going up. Chapels may be shrinking but sports stadiums are expanding. Don't get me wrong, entertainment and home improvement are fine in themselves, but become twisted when they receive the devotion rightly reserved for God, and consuming our time and money.

But the evidence of idolatry can be more subtle than that, and it is in its subtlety that its power lies. For instance, Nancy Clark has suggested that for many the contemporary interest in physical exercise is not simply a way of achieving health but is a kind of secular religion. She writes: 'As churches empty, health clubs flourish; as traditional fervour wanes, attention to the body waxes. In other words, as the baby boomers reach middle age, a yearning towards perpetual youth flares up and denial of the biological takes the form of aerobics' (*Faith in the Flesh* – Lynn Magazine, 1985). Of course, keeping fit is good, but what is the motivation? Is it that as good stewards we should care for the body which God has given us and not abuse it, or is it because all our thoughts are on this world, for we really don't think there is one beyond worth denying ourselves for, we have to do all we can to extend this life for this is the only shot we have? Is it that deep down we believe that the physical matters more than the spiritual? Maybe we should check ourselves at this point and ask ourselves how much we are willing to pay out for health club membership or cinema attendance, or a football season ticket compared to what we are often willing to give to the church? The former somehow has less of a sting to it.

The attraction of idolatry?
The first and most obvious reason why we are lured by idolatry is that we think it means we are not accountable to God because *we* have made the idol and so *we* feel *we* can control it. Notice the emphasis on *who* does the making in verses 12-15 – it is man who does the shaping or fashioning, a phrase which is repeated three times.

> [12]The blacksmith takes a tool
>   and works with it in the coals;
> *he* shapes an idol with hammers,
>   *he* forges it with the might of his arm.

He gets hungry and loses his strength;
    he drinks no water and grows faint.
[13]The carpenter measures with a line
    and makes an outline with a marker;
he roughs it out with chisels
    and marks it with compasses.
He shapes it in the form of man,
    of man in all his glory,
    that it may dwell in a shrine.
[14] He cut down cedars,
    or perhaps took a cypress or oak.
He let it grow among the trees of the forest,
    or planted a pine, and the rain made it grow.
[15]It is man's fuel for burning;
    some of it he takes and warms himself,
    he kindles a fire and bakes bread.
But *he* also fashions a god and worships it;
    he makes an idol and bows down to it.

Idols are safe, predictable, and controllable, there to serve us rather than we them. Why, in verse 17 the plea to the idol is 'save us'. In short, the idols reflect the self which is on the throne of our hearts. We may want power and status – why? Because it makes us feel important – it is our idol. We may move from one sexual conquest to the next. Why? Because it makes us feel good – it is our idol. All the time it is self which is central.

But the second reason why idolatry is so attractive is because it seems to work. There is a pragmatic dimension. That is certainly how it would have appeared to these Jews and why God through the prophet has to go to such lengths to disabuse them of that thought. The Babylonians were the top dog nation and they attributed all their success to their gods. So why couldn't these Jews simply wake up and come to terms with reality? How could they, humiliated as they were, continue to insist that the LORD was supreme ruler and their gods were nothing? Didn't the facts speak for themselves?

As we look out on our world and the relative ineffectiveness of the church don't we feel the same? Of course we do. That is why some churches have decided to play the world at its own game. Credit cards allow us to have without having to wait, some evangelists offer divine results without having to wait, indeed without having to think. One church in Phoenix Arizona has been built like a country club and has an attendance of 10,000 on a Sunday. The secret? The church is drama. Here is a description given by David Wells: 'The preacher punctuates his sermons with eye-catching antics such as his own personal flight to heaven on invisible wires and the use of a chain saw to topple a tree to make a point.' The church has become a circus. But it works, that is, people are drawn in. But to what? A Christianised version of Disneyland. God is side-lined as he is in the rest of society and the self is pandered to. Talk of sin is out, that makes people feel bad. Talk of affirming the self is in –

that makes people feel good and that is what they want to hear – the idol speaks the words the worshippers want it to say. We think we have domesticated God.

The failure of idolatry

Ultimately, the idols fail us. That is the chief burden of Isaiah's diatribe against idolatry. The futility of idolatry beginning in verse 9 leads to its pathetic climax in verse 20, 'He feeds on ashes, a deluded heart misleads him; he cannot save himself, or say, "Is not this thing in my right hand a lie?" '

His heart, which has manufactured the idol in the first place, has misled him. He thought the idol would bring him satisfaction, feeding him, when in fact it has left nothing but the taste of ashes in his mouth. The idolater can't save himself, or help himself, with regard to the idols; he is totally hooked. He can't even see the thing to be a lie, he has been blinded. He is unable to think straight (v. 19).

[19]No one stops to think,
no one has the knowledge or understanding to
say,
'Half of it I used for fuel;
I even baked bread over its coals,
I roasted meat and I ate.
Shall I make a detestable thing from what is left?
Shall I bow down to a block of wood?'

Some wood was used for fire, some for making a god, but both the ash and the god are products of the same thing. You might as well pray to dead embers, the prophet implies. He thinks he holds the idol but in reality the idol holds him and he is its slave. He is slowly becoming like the idol he has made:

> They know nothing, they understand nothing; their eyes are plastered over so they cannot see, and their minds closed so they cannot understand (v. 18).

Does that not describe perfectly the situation of many in our society today? The gods we have been so busily pursuing have failed us. The sense of well-being promised is not lasting and the idols are exacting their price. Let me give one example: psychosocial disorders amongst young people. A few years ago, Sir Michael Rutter, Professor of Child and Adolescent Psychiatry in London, and David Smith, Professor of Criminology in Edinburgh, published a massive study which focused on disorders that are increasing in teenage years: crime, suicide, depression, anorexia, bulimia and alcohol and drug abuse. What was striking was that a major increase in these problems occurred in the golden era of low unemployment and rising living standards between 1950 and 1973. In Britain recorded crime amongst the young has increased tenfold from 1950–1993. So has alcohol consumption and alcohol-related behaviour problems. We can also add drug abuse and suicide – especially amongst young males, as well as depressive disorders. What are the causes? The authors agree that those amongst the poor and those living on the 'sink estates' are more likely to be criminal, depressed, etc, than those in more comfortable surroundings – yet it can't account for the rise in these problems amongst young people in general, because the rise was the most marked during the period of prosperity. We have been fed the lie that material well-being equals spiritual well-being – it does not. The humanistic dream of the likes of Polly Toynbee is turning into a nightmare, and yet in one of her columns in the *Radio Times* she was still churning out the same old tired cliché that the answer to teenage pregnancies is more abortions, with free contraception to be doled out at school like dolly mixtures. We have never had so much sex education as in the last few years (that is as far as technique is concerned), yet we have never had so many sexual problems. Why? Because no moral framework is on offer, except the principle of enjoy yourself and be careful – the idol of pleasure again.

As hinted in verse 13, to try and make an idol which is less than man is to devalue man, it is a grotesque thing to do:

The carpenter measures with a line
    and makes an outline with a marker;
he roughs it out with chisels
    and marks it with compasses.
He shapes it in the form of man,
    of man in all his glory,
      that it may dwell in a shrine.

Yet we are the image bearers of God in all his glory, and that cannot be transferred to some lesser thing, without our self-worth being damaged in the process and God himself being offended. We were made to be more than pleasure animals and work machines – we were made for a loving relationship with God through Jesus Christ. Idols always let us down, especially at the moment we need them most. When you are on your death bed facing eternity, what good will that big house do you then? What effect will that career for which you have sacrificed everything benefit you? They can't save you. Only Christ can.

The alternative to idolatry
Idolatry is living a lie. The lie which puts self or some ideology in the place of God and which sees this life as the *summum bonum* and offers a thousand and one ways of attaining it. It inflates human pride while destroying the human soul. The only way to counter the lie is with the truth:

'Remember these things, O Jacob,
for you are my servant, O Israel.
I have made you, you are my servant;
O Israel, I will not forget you.
I have swept away your offences like a cloud,
your sins like the morning mist.
Return to me,
for I have redeemed you' (vv. 21-22).

This whole section begins in verse 6 with a reminder of who God is – the first and the last – eternal, no one made him, and yet as Israel's King, he made them (v. 21). You can call on the idols to save until you are blue in the face and they will not be able to lift a finger to help – how can they? Yet this is the redeeming God who can wipe away every sin and guilt (v. 22). These idols know nothing, but the true God foretells what is to come, even the future is open to him:

7'Who then is like me? Let him proclaim it.
Let him declare and lay out before me
what has happened since I established my ancient
people,
and what is yet to come –
yes, let him foretell what will come.
8Do not tremble, do not be afraid.
Did I not proclaim this and foretell it long ago?
You are my witnesses. Is there any God besides
me?
No, there is no other Rock; I know not one'
(vv. 7-8).

The idols are so unreliable – made of wood which can topple, this God is the Rock which is immovable (v. 8) and upon whom we can depend entirely.

Observe that when God occupies his rightful place, when we return to him (v. 22) and he becomes the centre of our thoughts and goals in life, then everything else falls into its rightful place too. The things he has made, the stars in the heavens, or the trees in the forest were never meant to be worshipped – they were meant to testify to the one who is to be worshipped – their Creator (v. 23):

> Sing for joy, O heavens, for the LORD has done this;
>   shout aloud, O earth beneath.
> Burst into song, you mountains,
>   you forests and all your trees,
> for the LORD has redeemed Jacob,
>   he displays his glory in Israel.

Do you see the freedom which the true God gives in contrast to the slavery of idolatry? The Christian can celebrate the joy of sex, not as an end in itself but as a God-given gift for the mutual enrichment of husband and wife within marriage. Music can be enjoyed not as a mindless master but as a gift of the Creator who causes the heavens to sing. Food is not to be despised or greedily consumed but received with thanksgiving. These are truths the redeemed know and are to proclaim, and as they do, with Christ being the centre of their lives, the glory of the Lord is displayed amongst his people.

We live amongst idols but we do not have to be their slaves. Even more than Israel we have been set free to serve the One who put all idols clearly in their place, Jesus Christ, when he said, 'Seek first the kingdom of God and his righteousness and all these other things will be given to you as well' (Matt. 6:33).

Chapter 4

Promises, Promises – A Different Understanding of Marriage

Mark 10:2-12

²Some Pharisees came and tested him by asking, 'Is it lawful for a man to divorce his wife?'

³'What did Moses command you?' he replied.

⁴They said, 'Moses permitted a man to write a certificate of divorce and send her away.'

⁵'It was because your hearts were hard that Moses wrote you this law, ' Jesus replied. ⁶'But at the beginning of creation God "made them male and female". ⁷"For this reason a man will leave his father and mother and be united to his wife, ⁸and the two will become one flesh." So they are no longer two, but one. ⁹Therefore what God has joined together, let man not separate.'

¹⁰When they were in the house again, the disciples asked Jesus about this. ¹¹He answered, "Anyone who divorces his wife and marries another woman commits adultery against her. ¹²And if she divorces her husband and marries another man, she commits adultery."

It was a hit movie, with breathtaking scenery and two of the most well-known stars of Hollywood – Robert Redford and Meryl Streep. The film was *Out of Africa*. In one scene the two stars are sitting on the beach talking. She wants him to marry her. Redford's response is: 'Do you think I'll love you more because of a piece of paper?'

It has to be admitted that such a view of marriage is becoming increasingly popular. Marriage is seen as little more than a piece of paper, an empty, and some would say, expensive formality. Perhaps more articulately, and certainly more forcefully, Tania Kindersley in her book *Don't Ask Me*, puts the case against marriage in these terms:

> Love should exist for its own sake, not because of legal ties or ceremonial obligation. If I ever consider spending the rest of my life with one person, I should like him to stay for me, not because he said so in front of a crowd of people, not because divorce is expensive. If you can say to someone: 'Here is the door, it's open.' That is a real sign of love and trust. Surely that is real security?

The statistics support the contention that a significant shift is taking place away from the traditional view of marriage in the direction of cohabitation, that is a man and woman living together in sexual union without that union being formalised legally by marriage. In the early 1970s one in ten marriages were preceded by cohabitation, in the early 90s it was seven out of ten, now it is approaching four out of five. For most couples it is a transitory phase, so half of the cohabitations last less than two years. But also 52% of those living together do eventually get married. This obviously has an effect on the experience of children. Some 17% of babies born are now born to those couples cohabiting, and it is estimated that within the next year or so only half of all children will spend their entire childhood within a traditional married family. So, the times, as they say, are a changing.

It has to be recognised that some people decide to cohabit for what they consider to be the best of motives. Maybe some have experienced as children the traumas of divorce and so in wanting to avoid the mistake of their parents want to check things out first. Some for economic reasons feel it is the best option. But there is a better alternative – that of marriage. So often marriage doesn't get a good hearing because no one has ever taken the time to explain what it really involves, that it is far more than a piece of paper, it is something woven into the very fabric of our existence. Neither is it pointed out that living together can very often have its down-side. What is more, if marriage is something which God the loving Creator has instituted, then it follows it must be for our best. There are good pragmatic reasons for marriage.

We must not receive the mistaken impression that marriage is going out of style. It is still the case that 82% of 16–17-year-olds expect to marry and only 14% of people think it is an outmoded institution. As I began by referring to two actors, here is one actress who gives a big 'thumbs up' for marriage. Nanette Newman, who has been married for over forty years, says: 'It is terribly sad that today people think having the same husband for your whole life is dull. It's much more intriguing than having affairs.' Nonetheless, marriage is under considerable strain.

How are we to understand marriage as God intends while living in 'Babylon'? In Mark 10 – in discussing the question of divorce – Jesus takes us back to the very beginning of creation, quoting the Book of Genesis, for the foundation of the basic principles of the marriage relationship between men and women.

Created not manufactured
In verse 6, Jesus refers back to Genesis 1:27: 'But at the beginning of *creation* God made them male and female.' This is not simply how God planned it, this is the way God made it. It is not a social construct which we can unmake and remake, it is a divine institution, a way of being as much as the change of the seasons and the revolving of the planets. This is a very important point. For if marriage is merely a social construct it can be reconstructed into any other configuration we wish, as Beckwith and Koukl argue:

> When traditional marriage is merely a social construction, no principled reason keeps the state from permitting virtually any marital union. For example, marital agreements that include two brothers or sisters, a mother and a son, a father and a son, a mother and a daughter, or a grandfather and a grandson, would be consistent with the philosophical assumptions undergirding the same-sex marriage defence.

God had two purposes in mind which marriage is meant to fulfil.

In the first instance it is meant to be the place where we fulfil our natural desire for companionship. That is spelt out in Genesis 2:18 when having made Adam God said, 'It is not good for man to be alone.' That doesn't mean of course that the single life is never fulfilling – look at Jesus – or that every marriage is. But the setting in Genesis makes it quite clear that it is God's ideal provision for our inbuilt need for companionship at the deepest and most fundamental level of our being – having a 'better half.'

In the second place, the marriage relationship provides the ideal setting for having and raising children, providing the secure and stable environment in which they can grow and learn to act responsibly.

Personal commitment not just a social contract

Jesus continues in quoting Genesis when he says, 'For this reason a man will *leave* his father and mother and be *united* to his wife' (Mark 10:7). In marriage a new family unit is being established. What is more, the word for 'united' or 'cleave' suggests that passion and permanence should characterise marriage. It involves the clear understanding that whatever may happen in the future there is that determined commitment to remain faithful and stand by each other through thick and thin.

Implicit within this idea of 'leaving and cleaving' is that of making a promise – a vow. The Bible's word for it is *covenant*, which is the background to that key passage from Malachi 2:14: 'The LORD is acting as the witness between you and the wife of your youth ... she is your partner, the wife of your marriage *covenant*.' This idea might well contrast to the verse written in a Hallmark card: 'I can't promise forever. But I can promise you today.' What we have in those two contrasting statements are two mutually exclusive views of love. There is Hallmark love, the love of the twenty-first century, unsure, ephemeral, here today and who knows about tomorrow. It is a love which breeds insecurity for it places us at the mercy of the emotional highs or lows of the other person – they fall in love and they fall out of love. Not so the love of the wedding service. Here love is not a tribute, it is a promise, a voluntary, personal *commitment* to somebody. When the groom and the bride say 'I will' to each other, they don't mean 'I think you are the best looking babe or the beefiest hunk in the whole wide world!' We are not so much paying the other person a compliment as making a personal commitment – a pledge – I will be true to you. It is here that the movie line from *Out of Africa* completely misses the point of a marriage covenant, for such a covenant never claims to regulate love's intensity but only its security. The world cannot see that love which truly loves is willing to bind itself, is willing to promise, willingly pledges itself so that the other may stand securely in that love. Will this person still love me tomorrow? He or she has given their word – that should be enough.

Permanent not temporary

This leads us on to the next aspect of marriage, it is a permanent relationship: 'The two shall become one flesh. So they are no longer two, but one. Therefore, what God has joined together, let man not separate' (Mark 10:8). This is not just a human transaction, it is a divine union – joined *by God*. Before marriage, they were just two individuals; now committed to each other publicly and consummating their new relationship sexually, the two have become one – they have become a unity. What is more, this understanding sheds light on the nature of the sex act itself. Sexual intercourse both expresses and brings about a deep permanent union – emotionally, physically, indeed spiritually, if you will. Therefore, when sexual intercourse is engaged in outside the context of a permanent marriage commitment, it becomes a lie. Sexual intercourse speaks of one thing – lifelong loyalty; and yet the intention of intercourse outside of marriage is something else – temporary mutual enjoyment. That is what is wrong with fornication. As with all lies it damages people in the long run.

It is especially at this point that cohabitation seriously falls short of God's intentions. It is a private arrangement which lacks the public acknowledgement of commitment, so there is at least an implication that it is not a lifelong commitment; there is a sense of trying things out which if it doesn't meet the test means it can be ended as quickly as it started.

Public not private

In the fourth instance, marriage involves a legal dimension. As we have already seen, the context of Jesus' teaching on marriage is set within the context of a question about divorce. That in itself assumes some form of legal setting within which the marriage relationship takes place. Certainly marriage is more than a legal agreement, it is a commitment in love to one another expressed in those solemn vows before God and society, but it certainly isn't anything less than a legal relationship. That requirement of a marriage certificate by society isn't some petty piece of bureaucracy – it is for the protection and well-being of the couple concerned and society as a whole. For it declares that the spouses are no longer available for committed relationships with anyone else. It protects any children in the marriage, establishing their identity and the responsibilities of the parents to that child. By way of contrast cohabitation is a private arrangement and does not take into account the wider responsibilities of society. If, after a long period of cohabitation, a separation occurs, then the legal aspects become all the messier. What is more, generally speaking it is the woman who is left the worse off.

Simply the best

The facts bear out the contention that marriage is for the well-being of individuals, couples, children and society as a whole, again in stark contrast to cohabitation. What is referred to below are generalisations, and there will always be exceptions. We will always be able to point to, say, a couple living together who are happier and more faithful than a married couple we know. But that may well be the same as pointing to someone who smokes fifty cigarettes a day who is in better health than someone who doesn't smoke at all.

Take relationship stability for instance. Cohabiting couples are almost six times as likely to split up as those who are married. Even where there are children, half of the cohabiting couples part within ten years, compared to just one in eight of married parents. Do you see how important that so-called piece of paper is? It's not so much the paper, but what it represents – the promise of fidelity backed up by society. Another problem faced by those who were cohabiting and then split up, is the mixed reaction of their family and friends. Here is a quote from a man, whose partner of five years just walked out on him, which illustrates the problem only too well: 'The worst part of this has been the lack of sympathy. If we'd been married, everyone would have rallied round trying to help.'

God in his wisdom and love gave marriage for the well-being of children. It is now estimated that broken cohabitations are responsible for between a quarter and a half of single-parent families. There is an increasing amount of alarming evidence that break up of such partnerships and marriage is damaging to children, in that they are more likely (although this is not inevitable) to suffer from poor performance at school, fall ill, have behaviour problems and fall prey to solvent and drug abuse and end up in court. These statistics are referred to, not to alarm those of us in such a situation or to make us feel more guilty than we already feel, but to make us face up to the situation in which we find ourselves, and see that the way of Babylon is destructive and steps must be taken to reverse current trends.

Neither is cohabitation all that encouraging on the faithfulness front. In the 1994 Sexual Behaviour in Britain report, it was found that only 43% of cohabiting men reported monogamy over the last five years, 24% reported concurrent partnerships (several at once), in comparison with nearly 90% of married men who reported monogamy in the last five years.

Marriage is also good for your health in a way that living together is not. Research in California comparing differences between those who cohabited prior to marriage and those who did not found: 'Cohabitors experienced significantly more difficulty in their marriages with adultery, alcohol, drugs and independence than couples who had not cohabited.' And in spite of the scorn that the media may heap on those who hold a traditional view of sex within marriage, the evidence points the other way. One survey has shown that of 'traditionalists' (those who strongly believe sex is for marriage), 72% report high sexual satisfaction, that is 31% higher than unmarried non traditionalists, who take a more casual view towards sex outside marriage. The same survey notes that women who rate high on religion have more fun in bed. To quote: 'Not only did more of the highly religious women say that their sex lives are "very good", but they apparently did not have a lower expectation of what sex should be. Women who had sex only with their husbands, for instance, experienced orgasm twice as often as women with multiple partners.'

While one can point to such findings to affirm the intrinsic goodness of marriage, from another point of view such goodness cannot be conclusively demonstrated. There will always be those who for whatever reason (usually ideological) will question it. So Robert P. George and Gerard V. Bradley write:

> If the intrinsic value of marriage, knowledge (justice), or any other basic human good is to be affirmed, it must be grasped in non-inferential acts of understanding. Such acts require imaginative reflection on data provided by inclination and experience, as well as knowledge of empirical patterns, which underlie possibilities of action and achievement. The practical insight that marriage, for example, has its own intelligible point, and that marriage as one-flesh communion of persons is consummated and actualized in reproductive-type acts of spouses cannot be attained by someone who has no idea of what the terms mean; nor can it be attained, except with strenuous effort of imagination, by people, who, due to personal or cultural circumstances, have little acquaintance with actual marriages thus understood. For this reason, we believe that whatever undermines the sound understanding and practice of marriage in a culture – including ideologies hostile to that understanding and practice – makes it difficult for people to grasp the intrinsic value of marriage and marital intercourse' (The Georgetown Law Journal, 1995).

As our society becomes more and more like 'Babylon' it is going to be more difficult to appreciate, let alone desire, marriage.

However, those 'non inferential acts of

understanding' to which George and Bradley refer will be important in the Christian apologetic. Some of these have already been referred to. Harry Jaffa notes others: 'The family is the foundation of all friendship, as it is the foundation of community.... Morality comes to sight therefore as the relationship, first of all, of husband and wife, then of parents and children, and of brothers and sisters. From this it expands to include the extended family, the clan, the tribe, city, country, and at last mankind. Mankind as a whole is recognized by its generations, like a river which is one and the same while the ever-renewed cycles of death and birth flow on.'

An even more surprising source arguing for the greater social value of marriage is D. H. Lawrence:

> It is marriage perhaps, which has given man the best of his freedom, given him his little kingdom of his own within the big kingdom of the State, given him his foothold of independence on which to stand and resist an unjust State. Man and wife, a king and queen with one or two subjects and a few square yards of territory of their own: This, really, is marriage. It is true freedom because it is a true fulfilment for man, woman and children.

He goes on to warn interwar Britain of any attempts to weaken the marriage bond:

Make marriage in any serious degree unstable, dissoluble, destroy the permanency of marriage, and the church falls. Witness the enormous decline of the Church of England, the reason being that the Church is established upon the element of union in mankind ... the marriage-tie, the marriage-bond, take it which way you like, is the fundamental link in Christian society. Break it, and you will have to go back to the overwhelming dominance of the State, which existed before the Christian era. The Roman State was all powerful (*Apropos Lady Chatterley*).

That is precisely where we have arrived at today – the state is all powerful.

The delicate and glorious treatment of marriage given at the beginning of the Bible in Genesis, spoken of again in Malachi, reiterated by Jesus and upheld by present research shows that overall men, women and children fare best within marriage. They are generally healthier, happier and more fulfilled. And despite claims to the contrary, cohabitation is a poor substitute for marriage and an ineffective trial for marriage.

We need to get back to God's basic design. This means more than talk from the church, it means action. That is what God was expecting of Israel in Malachi's time and what he expects of the church today – 'Guard yourself in your spirit and do not break faith' (2:16). Congregations should seek to support and train those who can assist in marriage preparation as well as marriage renewal. And while the church will want to do all that it can to promote the ideal of marriage, it will also see itself as having a duty to support and bring Christ's healing to those who, for whatever reason, are suffering from the effects of separation. At the very least it will want to provide that wider church family support of grace and forgiveness and strength which can be found in Christ for them and their children. For marriage is not only a divine gift from our God, it is also a divine picture of God's grace, with Christ being our husband, and we the church being his beloved bride, as Paul tells us in Ephesians 5. He has pledged himself to us irrevocably. He has bled for us so that we might be his for all eternity, so that, as Paul says, we might be presented 'to himself as a radiant church, without stain or wrinkle or any other blemish, but holy and blameless'.

Chapter 5

The Next Generation

Deuteronomy 6:4–25

⁴Hear, O Israel: The LORD our God, the LORD is one. ⁵Love the LORD your God with all your heart and with all your soul and with all your strength. ⁶These commandments that I give you today are to be upon your hearts. ⁷Impress them on your children. Talk about them when you sit at home and when you walk along the road, when you lie down and when you get up. ⁸Tie them as symbols on your hands and bind them on your foreheads. ⁹Write them on the doorframes of your houses and on your gates.

¹⁰When the LORD your God brings you into the land he swore to your fathers, to Abraham, Isaac and Jacob, to give you – a land with large, flourishing cities you did not build, ¹¹houses filled with all kinds of good things you did not provide, wells you did not dig, and vineyards and olive groves you did not plant – then when you eat and are satisfied, ¹²be careful that you do not forget the LORD, who brought you out of Egypt, out of the land of slavery. ¹³Fear the LORD your God, serve him only and take your oaths in his name. ¹⁴Do not follow other gods, the gods of the peoples around you; ¹⁵for the LORD your God, who is among you, is a jealous God and his anger will burn against you, and he will destroy you from the face of the land. ¹⁶Do not test the LORD your God as you did at Massah. ¹⁷Be sure to keep the commands of the LORD your God and the stipulations and decrees he has given you. ¹⁸Do what is right and good in the LORD's sight, so that it may go well with you and you may go in and take over the good land that the LORD promised on oath to your forefathers, ¹⁹thrusting out all your enemies before

you, as the LORD said. [20]In the future, when your son asks you, 'What is the meaning of the stipulations, decrees and laws the LORD our God has commanded you?' [21]tell him: 'We were slaves of Pharaoh in Egypt, but the LORD brought us out of Egypt with a mighty hand. [22]Before our eyes the LORD sent miraculous signs and wonders – great and terrible – upon Egypt and Pharaoh and his whole household. [23]But he brought us out from there to bring us in and give us the land that he promised on oath to our forefathers. [24]The LORD commanded us to obey all these decrees and to fear the LORD our God, so that we might always prosper and be kept alive, as is the case today. [25]And if we are careful to obey all this law before the LORD our God, as he has commanded us, that will be our righteousness.

Stephanie was found by her parents one day with her eyes tightly closed and with an intense look of concentration on her face. She was meditating. This came as something of a surprise to her parents since this was not a practice with which the family was familiar. Stephanie had, in fact, learnt it at school as part of an educational programme entitled 'PUMSY: In Pursuit of Excellence'. In the programme there is a dragon called 'Friend'. And Friend teaches Pumsy that her mind is like a pool of water. There is a muddy mind, which tends to think negative thoughts, and a clear mind, which can solve all her problems by positive thinking. But the 'clear mind' doesn't sound like a mind at all, more like a power or person. So Friend tells

Pumsy: 'Your Clear Mind is the best friend you will ever have. It is always close to you and it will never leave you....' Doesn't that sound strangely familiar? It echoes religious language, the sort of language we might use with our children when we tell them that Jesus is the best friend they could ever have who will never leave them nor forsake them. But in essence PUMSY is much closer to pantheistic Hinduism than Christianity, or to be more precise, New Age with its eclectic mysticism, sold to teachers as a means of promoting self-esteem.

That example comes from the United States. Nonetheless, what that episode does illustrate is the fact that our children are being brought up in a culture which is not value-free, but a postmodern culture which is laden with values which are far from sympathetic to many of the values and standards we would espouse as Christians. In short, our children, like the rest of us, have to contend with the idolatries of Babylon. They too are engaged in a battle for the mind and so a battle for their souls.

The challenge, therefore, to those of us who are Christian parents or grandparents or those into whose care parents have entrusted their children as Christian teachers or youth leaders is this: how do we help these children not only to resist the enticing influences of the surrounding culture, but actively challenge them?

One passage in the Bible which is specifically designed to help us in this is Deuteronomy chapter 6.

Here Moses is addressing the next generation of those who came out of Egypt as they stand on the threshold of entering into the promised land. Their parents, with the exception of a handful like Joshua and Caleb, had forfeited their right to that land by failing to trust in God's promises. They rebelled and so perished in the barren heat of the desert. It would appear, therefore, that everything is down to these people – the future seems to rest upon their delicate shoulders. And as we look at the deteriorating state of our nation today in the midst of cultural and social decay, not to mention the spiritual malaise afflicting the churches, we might well feel the same way about our children. How will they fare? Is there a future? Well, God is only too aware that the greatest threat to the well-being of his people does not in the first instance come from outright opposition, but ideological corruption – the tendency to be seduced away from God by the prevailing beliefs and practices of those who currently occupy the land of Canaan or by the nations which surround it, hence verses 13-19:

> [13]Fear the LORD your God, serve him only and take your oaths in his name. [14]Do not follow other gods, the gods of the peoples around you; [15]for the LORD your God, who is among you, is a jealous God and

his anger will burn against you, and he will destroy you from the face of the land. [16]Do not test the LORD your God as you did at Massah. [17]Be sure to keep the commands of the LORD your God and the stipulations and decrees he has given you. [18]Do what is right and good in the LORD's sight, so that it may go well with you and you may go in and take over the good land that the LORD promised on oath to your forefathers, [19]thrusting out all your enemies before you, as the LORD said.

What possible hope is there that they can resist the prevailing thought forms and idolatries which inevitably appeal to their corrupted nature? What hope is there for our children to swim against the tide of materialism, hedonism and the new superstition which plagues our land? Only one answer is given – remaining close to God by adhering to the Word of God.

A Word from God

'Hear O Israel: The LORD our God, the LORD is one' (v. 4). This is the cornerstone of Israel's creed, called the Shema, from the Hebrew imperative 'Hear'. In contrast to all the other religions with their emphasis on *seeing* through idolatry or *feeling* through ecstatic experience, the true and living God reveals himself by a Word which is a matter of *hearing* and *believing*. It is this Word of revelation which is to determine and shape all our thoughts about him and how we are to respond rightly to him. And what is it that is revealed but that the LORD – Yahweh – who is ruler over all and is the personal God who forms a loving relationship with his people in a covenant – that is what that name Yahweh means – he is one. In other words he is the ultimate reality which stands behind all other realities; what is right and what is wrong, what is beautiful and edifies and what is ugly and degrades. So the only way we are going to get our lives ordered aright is by getting our thinking about God right.

A Word for all

The first thing we notice about this Word from God is that it is for everyone 'Hear O *Israel*'. As God is indivisible in his being – one – so are his people Israel, the church. Therefore, God's revelation – the Bible – is not the private possession of a spiritual elite, it is to be accessible to all, from the youngest to the oldest. In fact, in this passage it is children, who are singled out in particular, upon whom this word is to be impressed in verse 7. However, it is to the adults that the command is addressed in the first place – verse 5: 'Love the LORD your God with all your heart, with all your soul and with all your strength. These commandments that I give you today are to be on *your* hearts.' Then comes verse 7: 'Impress them on *your* children.'

One thing children can spot a mile away is a

fake. If we are not taking God seriously, then why should they? But they will be impressed with the genuine article. As they see how important God is to us, meeting with his people regularly, valuing prayer, poring over his Word – what we *do* will reinforce what we *say*.

This is how the Christian writer, Don Carson, talks about how his parents' Christian lives had an impact on him and his sister as children:

> It was very difficult to get them to contradict each other, even though we children often did our best to drive a wedge between them, as children do, in the hope we could get our own way.... They pulled together in family discipline, avoided favouritism, and thereby made the home a secure and consistent shelter.... We grew up seeing Christianity at work. My parents weren't perfect; but more important they weren't hypocrites. They did not simply talk about the Lord, they put their faith to work ... they could not and doubtless would not shield us from the drunks who occasionally came to our table, from the difficult family situations with which they sometimes had to deal.... One of my most powerful memories concerns a Sunday morning when Dad had preached an evangelistic sermon in the church. After that service a curious little son crept up to the study door looking for his Daddy, only to discover him weeping and praying for some of the people to whom he had just preached. If in later years I had to learn to struggle with large questions of doubt and faith, truth and revelation, obedience and world view, at least I was never burdened with

a heritage of parental hypocrisy. My parents' faith was genuine and self-consistent; and there are few factors more important in the rearing and nurturing of children in a Christian home than this one.

The fact that it is the *whole* of our lives which testify to our children the reality of God underscores the truth that the Word of God addresses every part of our being, calling for a response of the whole person – heart, soul and strength (v. 5).

In order to love someone, we need to know them. Knowledge of God precedes love of God. If we and our children are to love God then we all need to grasp what he is like, what his priorities are, his likes and dislikes – and where does such knowledge come from? The Bible of course. And such a love in response is to come from the heart, which in Hebrew thought was not so much the seat of the emotions, but the very centre of our being. The heart is, if you will, the true self.

This too has implications for how we are to minister to our children. We must engage the whole person.

First, we must engage the mind at a level which is appropriate to them and in a way that will fire the imagination. If ever we give the impression that God is dull and Christianity is boring (although it has to be said there comes a stage in a child's life, round about the mid teens, when *everything* is boring, except saying everything is boring!) – then we have failed miserably because whatever God is as the One who is the Author of this amazing universe with all its diversity and wonder, he is far from boring.

What is more, we are to engage the emotions, while avoiding emotional*ism* which can be so manipulative, with its hype and attempt to bypass the mind in order to get children to do whatever we want them to do – the cheap 'decisions for Christ'. That is a deplorable practice which must be avoided at all costs. We must not lower ourselves to that, but we will want to put over the faith in such a way that the children respond with that unselfconscious spontaneity of theirs. So the church should use art and music and drama with children, setting up after-school groups and holiday clubs and so displaying the same creativity in getting over the gospel as our Creator God displays in shaping the world he has made.

A Word for all of life
Compartmentalism, dividing life up into the Christian and non-Christian is not an option for the Christian (vv. 6-9):

> [6]These commandments that I give you today are to be upon your hearts. [7]Impress them on your children. Talk about them when you sit at home and when you walk along the road, when you lie down and when you get up. [8]Tie them as symbols on your hands and bind them on your foreheads.

[9]Write them on the doorframes of your houses and on your gates.

Here we have the forceful reminder that the spiritual well-being of a child is primarily the parents' responsibility.

If you are a Christian father or a single Christian parent, you have your own little church over which you are to exercise pastoral care, it's called the family. And so without us becoming a bore, this passage does insist that we take, and make, every opportunity to relate God's Word to the world in which our children find themselves, helping them develop a *Christian* outlook on life, as it says in verse 7 – 'Talk about them when you are at home or when you walk along the road.' Not just in church once a week.

Here are just a few practical pieces of advice.

Start young. Some parents make the mistake of thinking that it is only when the children get a little older that they will 'introduce them to church'. No lower age limit is given here. I take it to mean that from the cradle we seek to share with our children the beliefs we have. This is not as silly as it may sound. The parent sings lullabies to the child in the cot, that have more than a soothing effect as they get older; why not sing some Christian lullabies? They exist. Also what about praying over the cot before you turn in for the night – both parents perhaps taking turns in doing this. And as they start to grow, invest in a children's Bible and there are some excellent children's Bible notes – spend time reading and praying with your child each night, make it a priority, and vary the prayers to make it an interesting and intimate experience. For you know, often that is the time the child will open up about what has happened that day at school, sharing their difficulties and pleasures. Include them in the prayer and so by example show how to thank God for his goodness and rely upon him for our worries. At the breakfast table before the meal, ask if there is anything which is especially going to happen that day to pray for – that is teaching the child that God cares about the whole of our lives, that he is the Lord, the one true God.

As the children get older still, you may want to let them in on your decision-making process, how you yourself as a family reach decisions from a Christian point of view, so that they learn what biblical principles apply and how. Look at verse 8: 'Tie them as symbols on your hands and bind them on your foreheads' – symbolising that God's Word is to affect our thinking – foreheads – and action – hands.

This is so important in a materialistic age like ours over the question of money. Is the way you view money and spend it any different from the unbeliever next door? It should be. This is how

Richard Forster puts it in his book *Money, Sex and Power*: he says that consciously or not we *will* teach our children about money:

> Our very reluctance teaches. Who we are and the daily transactions of life form the content of our teaching. Our children will pick up from us an all-pervasive attitude towards money: Should I fear money? Should I love money? Should I respect money? Should I hate money? Should I use money? Should I borrow money? Should I budget money? Should I sacrifice everything for money? All these questions and more are answered for our children as they watch us.... If we are free from the love of money, our children will know it. If apprehension is our automatic response to money, we will teach them worry and fear. Children need instruction in both the dark side and the light side of money. Without this, teaching them how to make a budget and write cheques is of little value.

That is right. If they don't learn from us the right attitude towards money and possessions, arising out of the Word, they will learn the wrong use from the world.

We are to start the day with God and end the day with God: 'when you lie down and when you get up' so that we live the rest of the day with God. Perhaps having watched something together on TV or having listened to the news on the radio, why not reflect on it from a Christian point of view, asking one or two strategic questions? It doesn't have to be anything deep, but it is attempting to cultivate a certain mind – set a habit of thought which is healthy. Christians are meant to view things in a distinctive way.

Furthermore, this love of God, which his people are to have, is to be shared with the wider community – as Moses puts it in verse 9: 'Write them on the door frames of your houses and on your gates.' Our profession of faith is not a private affair, it is public and we need to help our children see this too, so that they might be open about their faith to others.

A word for the future

In the future, when your son asks you, 'What is the meaning of the stipulations, decrees and laws the LORD our God has commanded you?' [21]tell him: 'We were slaves of Pharaoh in Egypt, but the LORD brought us out of Egypt with a mighty hand. [22]Before our eyes the LORD sent miraculous signs and wonders – great and terrible – upon Egypt and Pharaoh and his whole household. [23]But he brought us out from there to bring us in and give us the land that he promised on oath to our forefathers. [24]The LORD commanded us to obey all these decrees and to fear the LORD our God, so that we might always prosper and be kept alive, as is the case today. [25]And if we are careful to obey all this law before the LORD our God, as he has commanded us, that will be our righteousness' (vv. 20ff.).

The way in which faith is preserved and kept alive for future generations is by recounting to the next generation the saving action of the Lord. Do you realise that what you are doing when you pray with that child and share your faith with him, is not only going to be of eternal value for him, but could well be of eternal value to others, indeed, maybe changing the face of our nation? Think of it this way. That child now in your home or Sunday school group or youth club, is going to be so impressed by your love and devotion to Jesus Christ that she will marry a godly Christian man; they in turn will so impress their children, who will also have children, so that by the end of this century, from that family – which can be traced all the way back to your home – comes the next Billy Graham or John Wesley. Isn't that an amazing thought to have before us? God, you see, takes the long-term view with children. And so should we.

Chapter 6

Straight or Narrow?
Sexual Confusion

Genesis 2:18-25

¹⁸The LORD God said, 'It is not good for the man to be alone. I will make a helper suitable for him.'

¹⁹Now the LORD God had formed out of the ground all the beasts of the field and all the birds of the air. He brought them to the man to see what he would name them; and whatever the man called each living creature, that was its name. ²⁰So the man gave names to all the livestock, the birds of the air and all the beasts of the field.

But for Adam no suitable helper was found. ²¹So the LORD God caused the man to fall into a deep sleep; and while he was sleeping, he took one of the man's ribs and closed up the place with flesh. ²²Then the LORD God made a woman from the rib he had taken out of the man, and he brought her to the man.

²³The man said,

'This is now bone of my bones
    and flesh of my flesh;
she shall be called "woman",
    for she was taken out of man.'

²⁴For this reason a man will leave his father and mother and be united to his wife, and they will become one flesh.

²⁵The man and his wife were both naked, and they felt no shame.

It has been said that the first casualty of war is truth. That is certainly the case with the war which is at present raging all around us, although we may not be aware of it as such. I am referring to the ideological war which centres on the issue of sexuality, or more specifically, homosexuality.

We are considering what it is like to live as Christians in what the Bible calls 'Babylon' – a world which sets itself up in opposition to God and his ways. If we are to be effective ambassadors for Christ, then, like any ambassador on foreign soil, we need to understand two things. First, we need to understand the King we represent, that is, have our minds in tune with his wishes, values, aims and purposes and seek to promote them. For the Christian that means getting in touch with the mind of God through the Word of God – the Bible. That is where we discover our King's manifesto. But the second prerequisite is the need to understand the culture in which we have been placed, a culture which, as we have seen, is essentially hostile to the Kingdom we represent. Nowhere is this more so than in the arena of the sexual politics which practically consume our society.

But we must recognise that this liberalisation towards sex in the direction of almost 'anything goes', is part of a bigger shifting social landscape which may be leaving many of us feeling disorientated. It is a landscape where there are no fixed absolutes – everything is relative. It is a world in which we are told that truth is not so much discovered but created, we make our own truth. We live in a world of hype and spin. It is what the sociologists call a postmodern world – the old certainties are gone, everything is a quest for power, getting your own or your group's way. The Nietzschean dream (or nightmare) is being realised: 'This world is the will to power – and nothing else besides! And you yourselves are also this will to power – and nothing else besides!'

This is what has been happening to great effect during the last few decades in the area of homosexuality. The change has been remarkable. In the words of the psychoanalyst Charles Socarides we have seen a shift, 'from the love that dare not speak its name to the love that can't shut up – in barely 25 years.' In the early sixties it would have been political suicide for any cabinet minister to declare openly that he was a practising homosexual, he would immediately have become a social outcast. Such a thing seems ludicrous to us today. In fact the reverse is the case. To dare to raise a question about the moral legitimacy of homosexual practice brings with it public opprobrium and the charge of homophobia which ranks alongside racism and sexism as three great deadly sins in modern society.

Indeed, the most strenuous efforts are made to present homosexuality in the most favourable light possible. Not only is there *Gaytime TV*, or films like *Four Weddings and a Funeral* in which the only deep relationship is the one between the two gay characters, but which soap, whether it be *Eastenders* or the *Archers*, is without its resident homosexual, creating the impression that homosexuality is both common and socially acceptable with no down side at all? The discredited statistics of Kinsey that between one in ten and one in twenty men in society are homosexual still persists, and the cumulative effect of all of this is to practically foreclose on any rational public discussion about the gay issue for fear that those who would take a more critical, but caring stance, are liable to be pilloried as homophobic dinosaurs.

What is more, it has to be admitted that on the face of it, the argument for homosexual union sounds so reasonable. After all, why shouldn't two people who love each other and have a stable relationship engage in same sex union? What people do in the privacy of their own homes is their affair. Who are you to say it is wrong?

Before we look a little more closely at that question and see what light the Bible sheds on the answer, we need to remember some other words Jesus once said when he called his followers to be 'wise as serpents and innocent as doves' (Matt. 10:16). That is where Christians often fall down. We fail to have that shrewdness, that discernment, of what is happening around us, with the result that we get swept along with the prevailing culture, not realising what is happening before it's too late.

Let us, therefore, try and understand the big picture of where our society is coming from in order to see where it is going, and then contrast it with the big picture the Bible gives us of where creation has come from and where *it* is ultimately heading under God.

In her book *Sexual Politics* Kate Millett writes: 'The enormous social change involved in a sexual revolution is basically a matter of altered consciousness [i.e. slowly getting people to think differently], the exposure and elimination of social and psychological realities underlying political and cultural structures. We are speaking, then, of a cultural revolution.' That is what is happening. This doesn't mean that every actively homosexual person wants to attack traditional sexual patterns and ethics, but there is a basic cultural drift.

However, it has to be said that some groups are deliberately out to attack the family. Here is Bill Johnson, a practising homosexual clergyman and member of the Lesbian and Gay Christian movement: 'as long as the Church is able to perpetuate the belief that marriage and the family are the highest form of human relationship it will be able to perpetuate itself as a heterosexual family-orientated institution ... heterosexual relationships and marriage as traditionally experienced are basically unhealthy.' The Gay Liberation Front's 1979 manifesto bluntly stated that 'we must aim at the abolition of the family', and then went on to point out that the greatest defender of the family was Christianity. Of course, it is possible to move towards the abolition of the traditional family in other ways than by outright suppression. It can be eroded by saying there are 'alternative families', that the concept of family is more fluid, varied and open, as Joan Bakewell stated in her TV series, *My Generation*. This is why Section 28, which prohibits the promotion of homosexuality in schools, must be kept in England. (Or an alternative must be put in place.) This is not because there will be an immediate move in our schools to teach that homosexual relationships are good or better than heterosexual marriage, but because the pressure will be increased for it to be seen as a valid *option*, so adding to the moral confusion many are already experiencing, at a time when our young are so impressionable and vulnerable.

What are the facts?

First of all, homosexuality is not as common as we are often led to believe. Surveys in both Britain and America show that only 1% of men are exclusively homosexual, not 10%. That is the perspective we must have.

Secondly, the argument which is often put forward asking what is wrong with homosexual union in a loving stable relationship is, in reality, somewhat abstract and a red herring, for very few such *stable* homosexual relationships actually exist. The 1992 SIGMA study funded by the Medical Research Council found that 56% of actively homosexual men had 'open' relationships, and although 44% claimed a monogamous relationship, the average length of the relationship was only twenty-one months. The majority also had 'casual partners'. In any given year the number of casual partners was reported at between 0-300, with an average in the past year being seven, or to put it another way – one partner every seven weeks.

What is more, the 'stable loving relationship argument' undergirds the call for same-sex marriages. This is based on the assumption that marriage is simply a social construct. But if this is the case then why stop there? As Beckwith and Koukl argue: 'Nor is a polygamous marriage of one man and numerous spouses – which also may include his mother, his grandmother, his grandfather, as well as his adult daughter and son – inconsistent with the same-sex marriage worldview. Given sexual politics today, one can easily imagine polygamy being reintroduced by an appeal to the sad plight of the bisexual, a person who is incapable of fulfilling his or her marital aspirations with merely *one* spouse of *one* gender. The rhetorical question could be raised: Why should he or she be forbidden from marrying the *ones* he or she loves?'

Taking this line of thinking to its *reductio ad*

absurdum, they continue, 'Of course, we cannot ignore the marital rights of the person who has a deep and abiding affection for the family pet for then the animal rights crowd may pipe up and accuse us of *speciesism,* the prejudice favouring human beings over non-human animals.'

So, what harm is there? Far more than many would care to admit. Here are just some of the medical problems as referred to by Jeffrey Satinover: A 25–30 year decrease in life expectancy; chronic, potentially fatal, liver disease; infectious hepatitis; frequently fatal rectal cancer; multiple bowel and other infectious diseases; a higher than usual incidence of suicide; and the list goes on. To illustrate this specifically, in the *Journal of Death and Dying* the authors of an article analysed over 6,500 obituaries in the gay press in the USA over thirteen years and compared them with obituaries from two conventional newspapers. Those from conventional newspapers paralleled US averages in longevity – the median age of death for married men was seventy-five (with 80% dying aged sixty-five or over), for unmarried men it was fifty-seven (with 32% dying aged sixty-five or over). For over 6,500 homosexual deaths, the median age was thirty-nine if death was AIDS-related, and forty-two if from causes unrelated to AIDS. The authors conclude that: 'The pattern of early death evident in homosexual obituaries is consistent with the pattern exhibited in the published surveys of homosexuals and intravenous drug abusers.'

The general picture is tragically clear. There is very little that is gay or happy about such findings and our hearts must go out in compassion. To ignore such facts would be the height of irresponsibility, worse still is to affirm a gay lifestyle as being of equal validity to a married heterosexual one, as even some church leaders are now doing – that is bordering on the criminal.

But the objection is often raised: 'Surely, such same-sex attraction is normal for those concerned, whether it is the result of genetic or environmental factors is irrelevant, it is right for them.' Here a distinction has to be made between what is *normal* and what is *proper*. To say that something is acting *normally* is a matter of statistics, to say something is acting *properly* is a matter of design plan and purpose. For example, I might say that my car is acting normally if it starts after three turns of the ignition, but that is not what the manufacturer had in mind when he designed the car in the first place. What, then, is the Designer's plan for human beings? This is where the book of Genesis comes in.

The biblical view of sex and how we are to relate to each other isn't to be reduced to a few moral prohibitions. Even if there weren't any explicit passages which declared homosexual sex was wrong (and there are several), the Bible would still be just as clear on the subject because of all the positive things it has to say about *God's* intention for sex, or, if you will, the general ethos or attitude the Bible has towards sex. Kevin Vanhoozer puts the matter well when he writes:

> The biblical view of sexuality should not be reduced to moral prohibitions. The prohibitions against homosexuality only make sense against an overall sexual ethic and an overarching vision of what is good for humanity. With regard to sexual ethics, the Bible affirms heterosexual marriage as the good. The Bible's overall position on matters sexual is shaped by a positive vision of the good (e.g. by ethics) rather than negative prohibitions (e.g. by morality). That is, the Bible's aims for sexuality precedes its rules.

Here in Genesis we discover what that ethos and aims are, as well as some of the detailed specifications of how they are to be worked out.

First of all, sex is linked to reproduction which God declares as good (1:28):

> God blessed them and said to them, 'Be fruitful and increase in number; fill the earth and subdue it.'

This doesn't mean that every sexual act must issue in children, but it still remains as one of its primary purposes, what it is designed to achieve – all things being equal.

In the second place, in the picturesque account of the creation of man in Genesis 2:18 we are told that there was something which was not good, namely for man to be alone without a helper, that is someone who would complement him, be one with him and yet different. And having scoured the entire creation to find such a companion, it is at that point that God acts to bring a woman into being out of Adam's side:

> [20]But for Adam no suitable helper was found. [21]So the LORD God caused the man to fall into a deep sleep; and while he was sleeping, he took one of the man's ribs and closed up the place with flesh. [22]Then the LORD God made a woman from the rib he had taken out of the man, and he brought her to the man.

Here we have the principle of unity in difference – the two becoming one – psychologically, spiritually and physically – the coming together of, as it were, two halves to form a whole. This culminates, and is literally consummated in the act of sexual intercourse itself:

> [24]For this reason a man will leave his father and mother and be united to his wife, and they will become one flesh.

In other words, this is the design plan for sexuality – male and female. The activities of our bodies must fit the way we were made. Simply at the level of biological anatomy – the male and female were made for each other, not male for male or female for female. This is not an argument from biology to morality, but stating the obvious that biology testifies to the morality we have in the Bible.

This vital point, so often overlooked in the debate, is well summarised by David F. Wright:

> The sexual matching of male and female, which Christian tradition has always seen as rooted in God's ordering of the world he made, is embodied (literally) in the respective anatomies of man and woman. To put it bluntly, the penis and the vagina are "made for each other" in a way that is patently not true for the penis and any other orifice in the female body, let alone male body, or for the vagina and any other protuberance of the male – or female – body. That is to say, God's creative design for male and female to mate with each other is not airy-fairy theory, but a basic Christian belief that is borne out of the sort of human beings we are. It is a truth incarnated in our very flesh and blood.

The logical entailment of this is that it is impossible for homosexuals to engage in sexual intercourse with each other as Beckwith and Koukl contend: 'Since the purpose of sexuality is derived from our natures as men and women, homosexuals in the strictest sense are no more engaging in sex if they stimulate each other to orgasm than is an ashtray "food" and the act of "eating" if one consumes it.'

It is therefore clear that in the light of God's design and intentions for humanity, homosexual 'sex' is a disordered form of sex. It cuts across and frustrates the structures and purposes of God's creation. It actually undermines the uniqueness of heterosexual marriage, as do all other forms of disordered sex – fornication, rape and incest. This disordering is both a result of our rebellion against God, and an expression of it. That is the thrust of the apostle Paul's argument in Romans 1:24-28:

[24]Therefore God gave them over in the sinful desires of their hearts to sexual impurity for the degrading of their bodies with one another. [25]They exchanged the truth of God for a lie, and worshipped and served created things rather than the Creator – who is for ever praised. Amen.

[26]Because of this, God gave them over to shameful lusts. Even their women exchanged natural relations for unnatural ones. [27]In the same way the men also abandoned natural relations with women and were inflamed with lust for one another. Men committed indecent acts with other men, and received in themselves the due penalty for their perversion.

[28]Furthermore, since they did not think it worthwhile to retain the knowledge of God, he gave them over to a depraved mind, to do what ought not to be done.

Homosexuality, then, is against nature, not our own fallen, corrupted natures, but God's original intention and design.

A moment's reflection soon reveals why it is disordered.

In the first place, the element of complementarity is missing – unity in difference. What we have in the genital expression of homosexuality is an impossible attempted unity in sameness – the parts simply don't fit. This also has important implications for Christian theology and how we are to conceive of God's relationship to his people. So writes Vanhoozer: 'Even a loving relationship between two men fails to illustrate the nature of the relationship between God and his people, as marriage is supposed to do. The husband-wife relation, a relation of unity-in-difference, better pictures the relation between Christ and his church.' (cf. Eph. 5:22-33)

In the second place procreation is an impossibility – that is why surrogate mothers have to be sought for gay couples to have children, a necessity which ironically affirms all the more the abnormality of it all.

Sometimes the advocates of same-sex unions attempt to sidestep this objection by drawing a parallel between homosexual couples/ heterosexual couples who either decide not to have children or cannot have children for whatever reason. It is argued that one would not think of their marriage as being any less a marriage because procreation is ruled out, so why not allow for same-sex union which does not involve childbearing? Beckwith and Koukl's reply to this line of reasoning is worth quoting at length:

> The argument against same-sex marriage is based on the *nature* of human persons as beings with a gender who have a purpose derived from that nature. That is to say, male human persons are meant for coupling with female human persons, even if their coupling does not result in procreation. This argument is not based on a human person's *function, ability or desire*, which could each be inconsistent with how human persons ought to be by nature.... For example, a person who is comatose, insane, sightless, or sexually desirous of his neighbour's young child lacks something either physically, psychologically or morally. But he remains a human person who by nature ought to be conscious, sane, seeing, and desiring well. In the same way a sterile, aged, or willingly childless person is still a gendered human person whose purpose for marital union (unless called to celibacy) can only be consummated by one-flesh communion with a spouse of the opposite gender even if he or she has contrary desires.

One long-standing test for deciding upon a course of moral action is Kant's *categorical imperative* which, put simply, is this: Would you want everyone in the world to do it? We might therefore ask, would you want everyone in the world to be kind and generous? Would you will for everyone not to show hatred and prejudice and so on? The answer is yes. But, would you want everyone in the world to be homosexual? The answer is obviously 'No', for at the very least it would mean the end of the human race in terms of the survival of the species. It is not a universal good.

However, the God we worship is not simply the God who is our Creator and knows how we best function according to his design, he is also the God who is our redeemer and has intervened in this terribly disordered world to save us through his Son Jesus. Here are the words of the apostle Paul in 1 Corinthians 6:9-11, and note that the more socially acceptable sin of greed is right up there with sexual sin:

> Do you not know that the wicked will not inherit the kingdom of God? Do not be deceived: Neither the sexually immoral nor idolaters nor adulterers nor male prostitutes nor homosexual offenders [10]nor thieves nor the greedy nor drunkards nor slanderers nor swindlers will inherit the kingdom of God. [11]And *that is what some of you were*. But you were washed, you were sanctified, you were justified in the name of the Lord Jesus Christ and by the Spirit of our God.

Do we realise what that means? It means that the church is not a 'no go area' for those men and women who have a same sex orientation any more than it is a no go area for those of us who have greedy, or alcoholic or adulterous inclinations. Certainly there is no question of affirming any of these things as acceptable lifestyles, because in Christ we are called to an alternative lifestyle – a Christian one. Yes, we will continue to wrestle with our fallen feelings and all the temptations they bring until we go to be with Christ in glory, but we do not wrestle alone. We do have God's Spirit, God's Word, and the fellowship of God's people.

The gospel is for all without distinction.

Let me close with words from someone who was locked into a gay lifestyle, but then became a Christian:

We must not rewrite or water down the Scriptures. The Bible clearly states that heterosexuality is God's intent for humankind. It also presents all sexual behaviour outside of marriage as sin and not God's best for us. When I came out of the gay community I was looking for truth and direction. My gay friends said I was a fool. The church could only put homosexual people down and had no idea how to assist in the process of recovery. I found my direction from the Bible. It was the only safe place to go. The Bible gave me a true picture of God as a Father, his unconditional love for all his children, regardless of their struggles. My own father had not been able to parent me as I needed, the church had not been able to supply unconditional acceptance of me, but I found through the Scriptures that God would do these things for me. I learned healthy boundaries from reading the Scriptures. It was there I learned the things I needed to function in a whole way.... I shudder to think what may have happened to me if I had gone to a counsellor or church which had affirmed me in my homosexuality. If that had happened I may well have been dead from AIDS now. Many of the people I knew back then are now dead.

But then he goes on to say this, which I personally would want to underscore:

To many Christians who are struggling with unwanted homosexual feelings, I would say to you: there is hope and healing for you ... you are not a second class Christian. Jesus' death on the cross was for you as well. God is not ashamed of you. He is your Father and longs to lavish his love on you. You are not an unwanted child. Your life can be a testimony to the grace and healing love of your Father, so walk proudly into the glorious riches and the full inheritance that God has for all his children.

Chapter 7

Glittering Images

³³'No one lights a lamp and puts it in a place where it will be hidden, or under a bowl. Instead he puts it on its stand, so that those who come in may see the light. ³⁴Your eye is the lamp of your body. When your eyes are good, your whole body also is full of light. But when they are bad, your body also is full of darkness. ³⁵See to it, then, that the light within you is not darkness. ³⁶Therefore, if your whole body is full of light, and no part of it dark, it will be completely lighted, as when the light of a lamp shines on you.'

³⁷When Jesus had finished speaking, a Pharisee invited him to eat with him; so he went in and reclined at the table. ³⁸But the Pharisee, noticing that Jesus did not first wash before the meal, was surprised. ³⁹Then the Lord said to him, 'Now then, you Pharisees clean the outside of the cup and dish, but inside you are full of greed and wickedness. ⁴⁰You foolish people! Did not the one who made the outside make the inside also? ⁴¹But give what is inside the dish to the poor, and everything will be clean for you.

⁴²'Woe to you Pharisees, because you give God a tenth of your mint, rue and all other kinds of garden herbs, but you neglect justice and the love of God. You should have practised the latter without leaving the former undone.

⁴³'Woe to you Pharisees, because you love the most important seats in the synagogues and greetings in the marketplaces.

⁴⁴'Woe to you, because you are like unmarked graves, which men walk over without knowing it.'

⁴⁵One of the experts in the law answered him,

'Teacher, when you say these things, you insult us also.' ⁴⁶Jesus replied, 'And you experts in the law, woe to you, because you load people down with burdens they can hardly carry, and you yourselves will not lift one finger to help them.

⁴⁷'Woe to you, because you build tombs for the prophets, and it was your forefathers who killed them. ⁴⁸So you testify that you approve of what your forefathers did; they killed the prophets, and you build their tombs. ⁴⁹Because of this, God in his wisdom said, "I will send them prophets and apostles, some of whom they will kill and others they will persecute." ⁵⁰Therefore this generation will be held responsible for the blood of all the prophets that has been shed since the beginning of the world, ⁵¹from the blood of Abel to the blood of Zechariah, who was killed between the altar and the sanctuary. Yes, I tell you, this generation will be held responsible for it all.

⁵²'Woe to you experts in the law, because you have taken away the key to knowledge. You yourselves have not entered, and you have hindered those who were entering.'

⁵³When Jesus left there, the Pharisees and the teachers of the law began to oppose him fiercely and to besiege him with questions, ⁵⁴waiting to catch him in something he might say.

12 ¹Meanwhile, when a crowd of many thousands had gathered, so that they were trampling on one another, Jesus began to speak first to his disciples, saying: 'Be on your guard against the yeast of the Pharisees, which is hypocrisy. ²There is nothing concealed that will not be disclosed, or hidden that will not be made known. ³What you have said in the dark will be heard in the daylight, and what you have whispered in the ear in the inner rooms will be proclaimed from the roofs.'

'Advertising,' says the cynic, 'is the art of getting people to buy what they don't need by describing it in ways they know are not true.' Many would sympathise with that definition. Today, advertising is more than big business – it is a way of life. For, what is most commonly associated with advertising is now the very thing which shapes the way many people look and behave. That something is *style*. As Os Guinness has pointed out, 'style is *self*-advertising'. To choose a certain style is to choose a certain image we want to project. Identity – who we are – merges into image – what we want to appear to be.

The dominance of style found its zenith in the fashion industry as vaunted by Diana Vreeland, editor of *Vogue*. Her motto was 'fake it, fake it'. 'Never mind about the facts,' she used to say, 'project the image to the public.' The art of success, according to Vreeland, is to create a world 'as you feel it to be, as you wish it to be, as you wish it into being'.

Of course, the person who has elevated style to the level of a new art form is Madonna. She lives out the cliché that the medium is the message. She has total control over her shows, she writes the songs, produces the music, choreographs the dances, designs the stage set and even does her own make-up and costumes. Richard Morrison of the *Times* says this about her: 'The likes of Madonna and Jackson aim to offer what can only be called the total egocentric experience: they control every aspect of their acts and are willing to dissolve the line where art ends and reality begins...'. In other words, for Madonna, image and reality coalesce so one is very difficult to distinguish from the other.

Madonna is not alone. The surrender of reality to image, the sacrifice of personal integrity for the sake of public reputation, is a danger we all constantly face and, to which, we all in some measure succumb.

The motivation behind the concern for image is often pride and the consequence is deceit, that of others and indeed, self. This is the terrible trio which characterises Babylon, a world in organised revolt against God: 'In her heart she boasts, "I sit as queen; I am not a widow, and I will never mourn"' (Rev. 18:7).

Os Guinness writes: 'In a world in which first impressions may be the only impressions, we have to "sell ourselves on sight". In such a world of appearances, character loses significance, "face value" becomes all important, and the door is opened to the "make-over era" of spin-doctors and plastic surgeons.'

Nowhere is the danger of the dominance of

the false image more insidious than amongst religious people and especially those in leadership positions within the church. In fact Jesus spoke of it. He didn't call it the dangers of 'style' or 'spin', he spoke of the danger of the 'yeast of the Pharisees which is hypocrisy'. But, as we shall see, it is the same thing but only transferred from the arena of fashion to the arena of religion.

The very term 'hypocrite' itself originated in the world of the theatre, referring to the various masks a performer would wear according to the role he was playing. But the danger for religious people, and more specifically, pastors, is that the mask can become fixed – the public image mistaken for the inner reality. And the result is disastrous – we live a lie, we sincerely think we are something other than we are.

The cause of hypocrisy

[33]'No one lights a lamp and puts it in a place where it will be hidden, or under a bowl. Instead he puts it on its stand, so that those who come in may see the light. [34]Your eye is the lamp of your body. When your eyes are good, your whole body also is full of light. But when they are bad, your body also is full of darkness. [35]See to it, then, that the light within you is not darkness. [36]Therefore, if your whole body is full of light, and no part of it dark, it will be completely lighted, as when the light of a lamp shines on you.'

The cause is suggested by these two parables of Jesus. By talking about the function of the lamp to illumine a house and the eyes being the lamp of the body, Jesus is stressing the importance of the inner person being open to the wholesome, illuminating effect of the truth. If you deliberately switch off the light source, as when you put a lamp under a bowl, or fail to keep the eyes open and in good order, then sooner or later the inner personality is going to become morally darkened, incapable of discerning the show from the real thing. Playing the actor, therefore, is part of a spiritual benighting process which begins when we start to turn away from God's true light source, his own revelation of himself to us in Christ and his Word.

We are not to think that we wilfully start out with this intention. It can happen when the Bible becomes more of a source book for our sermons than for our own personal devotions. The pressure is on to keep on producing the goods for the pulpit rather than enriching that personal walk with the Lord; after all, people do not see ministers in their studies alone, but they do see them in their churches on public display. The result is a gradual eroding of the soul, particularly if we hide ourselves from certain aspects of scriptural truth which challenge aspects of our lives that we would prefer to keep hidden. The key cause of hypocrisy, then, is lack of personal integrity, the unwillingness to face up to the truth about ourselves because we are too busy trying to see how that truth applies to others. It is much easier to hide behind the religious mask of the omnicompetent successful minister.

The characteristics of hypocrisy

[37]When Jesus had finished speaking, a Pharisee invited him to eat with him; so he went in and reclined at the table. [38]But the Pharisee, noticing that Jesus did not first wash before the meal, was surprised. [39]Then the Lord said to him, 'Now then, you Pharisees clean the outside of the cup and dish, but inside you are full of greed and wickedness.'

Jesus here engages with two distinct but related groups of people – the Pharisees (v. 38), and the scribes, the experts in the Jewish law (v. 45).

As we know, the Pharisees were a group of lay fundamentalist enthusiasts. They were committed to the teaching of Scripture and its application. So much so that they developed a whole system of rules and regulations to make obedience to Scripture possible – so they thought. We often picture the Pharisees as those who wanted to make the law difficult; on the contrary, they wanted to make it easy – liveable. They longed for that assurance that they had kept God's law. There was to be no room for doubt for them. They took their religion seriously and they wanted others to take it seriously too. If they were around today and members of the Christian church instead of the Jewish synagogue, where would we expect to find them but in those groupings which promote their faith, which have a zeal for mission and are terribly concerned with the moral state of society.

On the other hand, the experts in the law were more like professional theologians and ethicists. If there was a dispute of biblical interpretation – they would be the ones you would consult for a resolution. Today you would find them on the board of some of our academic theological institutions.

The danger of hypocrisy, therefore, is one which is a special snare for those who want to take their belief seriously. So, we had better watch out – Jesus says so in 12:1. It is to the *disciples*, not the crowd, he says, 'Be on your guard against the yeast of the Pharisees.' It begins as a small thing, like yeast, but also like yeast its effect is all-pervasive and totally disproportionate to its size.

The first characteristic of hypocrisy is its concern with *external appearance at the expense of internal character* (vv. 39-41):

³⁹Then the Lord said to him, 'Now then, you Pharisees clean the outside of the cup and dish, but inside you are full of greed and wickedness. ⁴⁰You foolish people! Did not the one who made the

outside make the inside also? ⁴¹But give what is inside the dish to the poor, and everything will be clean for you.'

The background to this of course is the Mosaic prescription that certain vessels be cleansed to offset ceremonial defilement. The scribes added to what Moses laid down and went into overdrive. They were scrupulous in this. Jesus wasn't, hence the surprise in verse 38. He dispensed with it. Why? Well, Jesus saw the principle clearly: God is creator not only of the externals of a person – the image – but the inner character as well – the substance. The sort of piety he is looking for is not religious rigmarole but moral kindness – a sacrificial giving to the poor for instance. God is not only looking for clean hands but a clean heart. This is never lurking too far away from our own door. Think of the greater concern the church council can show over the state of the church pews than the moral state of our own lives, or whether the young person coming to our church is wearing a tie or has the right accent – rather than the fact that shabbily dressed though he may be, he is at least trying to care for the poor and needy. Concern with image, not reality.

Secondly, hypocrisy is *concerned with small legalistic details to the detriment of major moral issues* (v. 42):

Woe to you Pharisees, because you give God a tenth of your mint, rue and all other kinds of garden herbs, but you neglect justice and the love of God. You should have practiced the latter without leaving the former undone.

In the Old Testament God required his people to give a tenth of their income. But what was not included within that prescription was the herbs grown in your garden. Not so, however, for the religiously devoted. After all, they were *committed* believers: God can have a tenth of that too. And so we have this absurd cartoon of the Pharisee beavering away in his kitchen counting out every tenth mint leaf – 'that is for God', he would say proudly. This obsessional attention to detail can in some cases be symptomatic of a deep neurosis – washing hands three times before a meal, turning the light on and off four times before entering a room, arranging socks on the bed in a certain order. Why? In some cases it has a vicarious effect, a means of handling guilt. An easy way of making sure we are on the right side is by keeping the little rituals of our own design. That is much easier than concerning oneself with the bigger issues like social justice or love of God. Distract yourself from real moral failure by focusing on ritual. Again who has not seen it or fallen prey to it? It is much easier to make sure we 'take our communion', sing our statutory three choruses or be meticulous in our Bible study than it is to show *sacrificial* love to God and neighbour.

Which brings us to the next characteristic of the religious self-advert and that is the *concern with gaining public applause to the neglect of positive moral influence*:

> 43 Woe to you Pharisees, because you love the most important seats in the synagogues and greetings in the marketplaces.
> 44 Woe to you, because you are like unmarked graves, which men walk over without knowing it.

Do you see how their whole spirituality was designed to impress? It was the American comedian, George Burns, who was once asked what was the secret of his long and successful career, to which he replied, 'When I learnt to fake sincerity, the rest was easy.' Everything about these people was one big self-advert of fake sincerity – sham religion which was mistaken for true piety. They sat at the front where they were noticed. Their prayers were long and impressive, their giving loud and extravagant, even their clothes marked them out as different and they loved their religious titles, being addressed as the equivalent of Vicar, Bishop or Pastor. They thrived on it, for it reinforced the image they were so desperate to convey.

But far from their piety being a blessing to others it was in fact a curse; they were, says Jesus like 'unmarked graves'. To touch or walk on a grave caused a Jew to become ceremonially unclean and so incapable of approaching God. Therefore, graves were clearly marked off. But when you came into contact with these people, thinking that their company would draw you closer to God, the very reverse took place, you became spiritually contaminated. How? Because you would naturally think their way was God's way, the spiritual way, and their lives models to emulate and in so doing you would copy their hypocrisy and fall foul of the curses Jesus pronounces.

Let us consider: Is there anything that comes closer to a performance than preaching? Is there anything that resembles an audience more than a congregation? There is that temptation to think that provided the sermon has been on form, the accolade 'Good sermon Pastor' has been received, we can bathe in the warm glow of success and a job well done. And how awful the feeling if that compliment is not forthcoming. As Richard Baxter pointed out in his *Reformed Pastor*, many a sermon's throat has been effectively cut by the ill temperate behaviour of a preacher who, for all his impressive rhetoric, exhibits none of the graces he enjoins upon others. What did Ghandi say? 'We would all be Christians if it weren't for the Christians.'

We may well think that is enough. But Jesus relentlessly presses his point home, this time with the scribes in his sights (v. 46):

Jesus replied, 'And you experts in the law, woe to you, because you load people down with burdens they can hardly carry, and you yourselves will not lift one finger to help them.'

In their case hypocrisy makes religion arduous and unacceptable. It is all a list of 'dos' and 'don'ts'. According to Psalm 19 the study of the Bible should be a wonderful delight, but they had turned it into a laborious chore. Why? Because they were lawyers, the professional Bible interpreters, and, obviously, the more complicated they made biblical interpretation the more indispensible they became and so all the more important.

Again does not the church need to take stock at this point to discern how much of 'Babylon' has seeped into our thinking? In the minister's handling of the Scripture, what is it he is trying to do? Is it to demonstrate how clever he is, what books have been read, which authorities can be quoted, so people go away thinking what a remarkable person he is and how they could never do anything like that? Consequently the pedestal is raised one notch higher. Or are they, in another respect, trying to save themselves from the need of thinking? So, if they can follow what is being said, how the minister has arrived at that point, they can say, 'Of course, I should have seen that.' In their presentation of the faith is the impression given that it is a delight or a dour business because that seems all the more spiritual – and so in reality ministers become a stumbling block?

There is a story of a woman whose teenage son showed no interest in Christianity whatsoever. She would nag him to go to church, leave tracts on his pillow, place Bible verses in his lunch box, all to no avail. One day in despair she dropped to her knees and prayed: 'Dear Lord, whatever the obstacle is to my son becoming a Christian, please remove it.' Suddenly there was a flash of lightning and she completely disappeared!

Even worse, hypocrisy makes *religion intolerant and incapable of change*:

> [47]Woe to you, because you build tombs for the prophets, and it was your forefathers who killed them. [48]So you testify that you approve of what your forefathers did; they killed the prophets, and you build their tombs. [49]Because of this, God in his wisdom said, 'I will send them prophets and apostles, some of whom they will kill and others they will persecute.' [50]Therefore this generation will be held responsible for the blood of all the prophets that has been shed since the beginning of the world, [51]from the blood of Abel to the blood of Zechariah, who was killed between the altar and the sanctuary. Yes, I tell you, this generation will be held responsible for it all.

These people made a living out of Scripture but what they were not willing to do was to tolerate the living voice of Scripture – the Word prophetically applied. They were quite happy to canonise dead preachers, but they were not willing to listen to live ones. The same is true today. How many Methodists are happy to sing Wesley's hymns but would baulk at his beliefs about Heaven and Hell and the need for conversion? How many of those of us who would proudly own the name evangelical, and enthusiastically subscribe to the belief in the infallibility of Scripture none the less kill it dead by presenting it in a way which is, to be honest, plain antiquated with no contemporary application – locked in by the particular tradition in which we find ourselves? Others of us because of fear of charismatic excess preach as if the one thing the Holy Spirit must disapprove of is emotion! For every one finger pointing at others there are three pointing back at ourselves.

But worst of all, according to Jesus, concern for style – public acceptability – *makes saving truth inaccessible* (v. 52):

> Woe to you experts in the law, because you have taken away the key to knowledge. You yourselves have not entered, and you have hindered those who were entering.

They have locked the door on the kingdom of God and have thrown away the key. By their addition to Scripture and the complication of

Scripture, the message of Scripture has been obscured. It was said of men like Alan Stibbs and J. I. Packer that they sacrificed their academic reputation for the sake of the gospel; holding to their views they ensured that they did not gain a place in the hallowed halls of academia, although they were certainly most able. Today we see a different phenomenon, men sacrificing the gospel for the sake of their reputation. Don Carson relates the story of a notable English evangelical academic whom he invited to contribute to a symposium he was editing on Scripture and Truth. He declined. The reason he gave was that if he accepted, it might hinder his influence in the wider academic community. Sadly, it has to be said, that several years on, this person has seriously undermined one of the central gospel truths through his writings. But do you see where the temptation comes from? To be seen to have the right image; and so one must not be too closely associated with a certain brand of evangelicalism.

But we must ask to what extent do we as evangelicals contribute to creating a culture of hypocrisy which is the culture of Babylon? For instance, what do we consider to be a good model for ministry – in practice? Is it not still the omnicompetent all self-sufficient man or woman at the front? We simply must have our evangelical super-heroes as a breed apart. Not surprisingly those placed in such a position often seem isolated

– indeed aloof, for it all adds to that mystique of being different as folk we can look up to. In part this is a response to expectations, in part it is self-imposed – an essential element in the ministerial self-protection mechanism. We don't want to get too close to such ministers because we might have our own illusions shattered, discovering they are really like the rest of us. On the other hand, they don't want to get too close to us because then their image and so ministry could be placed in jeopardy. In spite of such clichés that it is more important to be faithful than successful, when it comes down to it, success is such an important part of our evangelical ethos, and so fosters the hypocrisy Jesus condemns.

Just listen to the conversations which take place between ministers. When asked how are things going, they are always encouraged, listing all the positive things, no matter how forced. They feel they have to engage in this charade, for to admit of anything less brings their competence into question and the fear of exclusion from the club. Or else they look at the big churches, the successful ministers and the conference speakers and out of shame and failure they retreat quietly into a corner, taking a side glance in the mirror just to make sure the mask has not slipped.

We can so easily foster isolation amongst our leaders. Where can that leader go to if he is feeling the pull of sexual temptation, or experiencing the pressure of lack of money and the collection plate looks so inviting, or is only too aware of the stress which is so great that the bottle must be opened – only for one more drop to see him through? Does he speak to the elders? Hardly, they pay him. For Anglicans maybe he can go to the Bishop? Well, if the Bishop is a believer at all he is the one who has some pull on the minister's so-called career. Maybe another minister then? But even here, the advice is not always helpful and is often an attempt, albeit a sincere one, to fix the mask further.

Not too long ago I was speaking to a minister who had to go to his elders for a pay rise, since what he was getting was well below the rate of inflation. He was told by one of his leaders that he didn't think he deserved what he was getting already! So he turned to some senior evangelical ministers. The advice given was that it was vital for a minister to be poor for it kept him humble. One may ask: how is it that the elders are not so concerned about their own humility that they ensure their own income is low by giving more to the church? Here is hypocrisy which is compounded all the more by adding to the pressure on the minister to play the actor.

How many a minister's heart is simply breaking because he cannot keep up the image any longer? Such play acting is a lonely, crushing business anyhow.

The correction of hypocrisy

It is interesting how Madonna sees her present concern for presenting a successful image arising out of her own religious background. She says: 'My Catholic upbringing is probably the foundation of everything I do. Once you're a Catholic, you're always a Catholic in terms of feelings of guilt and remorse. Sometimes I am racked with guilt. You're always striving to be good.' Isn't that the problem and burden of style religion, even style *evangelical* religion – striving to be good? But of course, Jesus came precisely for those for whom this striving was proving impossible, who were tired of the pretence, whose mask had slipped and whose image in the mirror simply repulsed them. As Jesus points out in 12:4 it is fear which often drives people towards hypocrisy: 'I tell you, my friends, do not be afraid of those who kill the body and after that can do no more.' It is fear of other people, fear of failure and disapproval – 'his sermons are not as good as they used to be, he is not as sound as others or as entertaining.' The list and the attendant pressures are endless.

But Jesus offers a way out of this bondage and that is a sweet reverence for the one who does know our hearts, who sees behind the masks and remarkable as it may seem, still loves and cares for us – it is that unconditional grace:

6'Are not five sparrows sold for two pennies? Yet not one of them is forgotten by God. 7Indeed, the very hairs of your head are all numbered. Don't be afraid; you are worth more than many sparrows.'

Do we believe it?

Chapter 8

Brave New World

Isaiah 65:17-25

[17]'Behold, I will create
    new heavens and a new earth.
The former things will not be remembered,
    nor will they come to mind.
[18]But be glad and rejoice forever
    in what I will create,
for I will create Jerusalem to be a delight
    and its people a joy.
[19]I will rejoice over Jerusalem
    and take delight in my people;
the sound of weeping and of crying
    will be heard in it no more.

[20]'Never again will there be in it
    an infant who lives but a few days,
    or an old man who does not live out his years;
he who dies at a hundred
    will be thought a mere youth;
he who fails to reach a hundred
    will be considered accursed.
[21]They will build houses and dwell in them;
    they will plant vineyards and eat their fruit.
[22]No longer will they build houses and others live in them,
    or plant and others eat.

For as the days of a tree,
    so will be the days of my people;
my chosen ones will long enjoy
    the works of their hands.

²³They will not toil in vain
   or bear children doomed to misfortune;
for they will be a people blessed by the LORD,
   they and their descendants with them.
²⁴Before they call I will answer;
   while they are still speaking I will hear.
²⁵The wolf and the lamb will feed together,
   and the lion will eat straw like the ox,
   but dust will be the serpent's food.
They will neither harm nor destroy
   on all my holy mountain,'
      says the LORD.

In March 1997, thirty-nine members of a group known as the Heaven's Gate staged a bizarre mass suicide in an affluent community near San Diego, California. The cult members apparently believed that by taking their lives they would rendezvous with a spaceship hiding in the tail of comet Hale-Bopp, which was passing by Earth. The spaceship would then transport the faithful cult members to heaven.

At about the same time a poll was published which revealed that Canadians, who according to the UN Human Development Index, live in what the rest of the world finds to be the most desirable place on earth, are in fact 'in the grip of unprecedented national despair' and 'foresee a grim future' such that they have given up on traditional institutions such as government.

What future?

What these two news stories reveal in different ways is the fact that within Western society there is an increasing uncertainty about the future. As Woody Allen once said: 'The future isn't what it used to be.' And that is so. Not all that long ago the prevailing belief of many of our grandparents and great-grandparents was that through a combination of education, technology and moral enlightenment, Utopia was going to be achievable by the end of the twentieth century. So Desmond King-Hele concluded his book *The End of the 20th Century* with these words:

'If war is avoided, if the hungry are fed, if the rise of the population is checked and the quality of living is improved by curbing pollution and building new towns to live in, we might advance to a marvellously fruitful era when the future wonders of science and technology will be exploited for the benefit of all.'

Did you notice how many 'ifs' are in there? As we begin a new century we are left with such words ringing hollow in our ears.

In many ways the song from the musical film *Paint Your Wagon* is a fitting anthem for our generation: 'Where am I going? I don't know. Where am I heading? I ain't certain. All that I know is I am on my way.' We still hear, don't we, talk of progress through technological advance. The problem is, we don't quite know where we are going. Our civilization was not born under a wandering star but a shooting star, which seems to be plummeting to a sudden end. Not surprisingly we may be the first generation to be living without hope, being devoid of any belief which will enable us to live in the present by having a clear view of the future. In a novel by Douglas Coupland, one character expresses such anxiety about the future in this way: 'There's a darkness to the future ... the future's not a good place' (*Girlfriend in a Coma*). Maybe that is why so many people live for the 'now' – living on easy credit and 'partying' – don't worry about tomorrow for there may well not be one. Whereas at one time the future was rosy, now the future is merely orange.

But there is one group of people on this planet who above everything else are people of hope, and that is Christian believers. For woven into the fabric of the Bible's story-line is that this world has an origin – in God, and also a future – in God. The one who has made the heavens and the earth by his Word will also make a new heaven and new earth by that same Word. In fact he has already begun the process by calling into being a new race who will populate this transformed cosmos and he does this by the Word of his gospel.

What we are given in Isaiah 65 is a glimpse into what that future entails. This would have been a message which would have meant so much to those exiles living by the rivers of Babylon. How much more will these words mean to those of us living in modern day Babylon?

Invariably figurative language is used; how else can the prophet describe the indescribable but by drawing on aspects of our present life to create impressions of the life to come? That is what these are; impressions to support our faith and not details to satisfy our curiosity. It will be a future, says Isaiah, in which we shall be totally happy (v. 19), totally secure (v. 22) and totally at peace (v. 24). So what the prophet does under the inspiration of God's Spirit is to draw upon our own present experiences and contrast them with what we shall experience when this glorious transformation takes place.

Cry freedom

The first thing about this new world order is that it is a place where there is *freedom from sin.* We are told in verse 19 that God will *rejoice* over his new Jerusalem and take *delight* in his people. Of course, God would not be able to do that if it contained any blemish, anything that spoiled or marred what he had made. Back in Genesis 1 we are told that when God created the heavens and the earth, he pronounced it very good. But this new creation is going to evoke from God more than a positive affirmation; it is going to draw forth from his heart rejoicing, sheer delight. This new city will be a delight and its people a joy, says Isaiah.

Now there is a contrast. For right at the beginning of this prophecy we have a description of Jerusalem and God's people which is anything but a delight. The city is a disgrace, a cesspool of moral corruption and decadence, people selfish and rebellious. Far from delighting God's heart they break it. Instead of evoking commendation they receive condemnation (Isaiah 1:21):

See how the faithful city
　　has become a harlot!
She once was full of justice;
　　righteousness used to dwell in her –
　　but now murderers!

In many ways that city represents our world on the run from its Maker – it has become like Babylon. So what the people will be taken to in captivity will befit them.

But what has happened between chapter 1 and chapter 65 to enable the prophet to look forward with confidence to a new city and a new people being brought into being? Just over half way through the book God promises to send his Servant whom we are told in chapter 53 was to be led like a lamb to the slaughter, to hang on a scaffold, upon whom God will lay the iniquities of us all, as a sacrificial guilt offering to bear away our sins.

In other words, redemption is promised (Isa. 53:4-6):

> ⁴Surely he took up our infirmities
>   and carried our sorrows,
> yet we considered him stricken by God,
>   smitten by him, and afflicted.
> ⁵But he was pierced for our transgressions,
>   he was crushed for our iniquities;
> the punishment that brought us peace was upon
>   him,
>   and by his wounds we are healed.
> ⁶We all, like sheep, have gone astray,
>   each of us has turned to his own way;
> and the LORD has laid on him
>   the iniquity of us all.

What we see here is the full fruits of that redemptive work, the formation of a renewed people whom God has purchased with his own blood to dwell with him into all eternity. Of course that has already happened – Jesus was that Servant. He is the Lord redeeming a people for himself and he is the one who is yet to come to establish his kingdom for ever. So, as with Isaiah we glimpse the future, we see a world in which the effects of sin are reversed, the old order of a world under the shadow of God's curse is replaced by a new world under the light of his blessing, because that which drew the curse, sin, is no more – it has been removed by Jesus.

'Never again will there be in it an infant who

lives but a few days or an old man who does not live out his years; he who dies at a hundred will be thought a mere youth' (v. 20). One of the most poignant and painful reminders that we live in a world which has gone badly wrong is death. Nowhere is this more shattering than with the death of an infant. I have had to conduct such funerals and I tell you frankly, it is devastating, for instinctively we cry out this should not be. In the days of Isaiah infant mortality was much higher than in ours: one could have four or five children in a family who would not reach adulthood. And even then to get beyond forty-five was a major achievement. We live in a world terrified of death – the taboo subject of the twenty-first century. Understandably so, for there is no answer to it. We might delay it but we cannot eradicate it. But that great terror will be no more in this new world. No infant will fail to enjoy life nor an elderly person come short of total fulfilment. In fact, you would be but a mere youth if you were to die at a hundred! This doesn't mean death will be present: it is simply a poetic way of saying that over the whole of life, young and old, the power of death will be destroyed.

The disharmony which characterises our world, the enmity within nature will be replaced with total unity – so as it says in verse 25 what were natural enemies – wolves and lambs – will lie down together. Even lions will become vegetarians. All that we can now only dream of will then become a reality.

But. . .
Two worrying questions which Christians often raise are answered in this passage.

The first is this: in Heaven, will it be possible for me to sin again? Have you ever wondered about that? If when the world was originally made perfect people sinned, could it not happen again in the new world? The short answer to that is, No. And here is the explanation.

In verse 24 we read these words: 'Before they call I will answer; while they are still speaking I will hear.' That means there is such complete oneness between God and his people that he anticipates their needs with a constant providential watchfulness. But more than that there is such an identity between them, that while the people are still speaking, what they say immediately commends itself to God, i.e. what they want and what he wants are one and the same. This is because in the new heaven and new earth we shall be given new hearts and new minds devoid of any sin, so we shall never be out of sync with God. We will not only not want to sin but not want to want to sin because we will be so reconstituted by God that we will be incapable of it.

It has to be admitted that this idea is totally unacceptable to the modern mind, even some

Christians who think of freedom as the ability to choose between different courses of action, between good and evil. But that is not the biblical view of freedom. Freedom is the ability to choose according to the truth, to do what you ought, not just what you want. And of course that was Jesus' position. He was tempted and felt the struggle, but he couldn't sin, he didn't want to. As Paul Helm has argued:

> if to have such a moral character that you cannot sin and do not want to sin means you are not free, then Jesus wasn't free, and neither is God for that matter for he *cannot* sin. But it is a miserable delusion and a pathetic concept of freedom to think that if only God could succumb to temptation he would be free and not otherwise. No, the glory of God, which makes him the supreme object worthy of our worship and total trust is that he is incapable of change, unable and unwilling to depart from the immaculate standards of his own majestic holiness.'

The wonderful gospel truth is that when we get to Heaven we will be like him in this respect – free to do only what is right and loving every minute of it!

The second worry we sometimes have is this: if, as we have seen in verse 19, heaven is a place of consummate joy, will not that joy be diminished and sullied by bad memories of what we have done on earth or by thoughts of those who are not in Heaven?

Look at the end of verse 17: 'The former things will not be remembered, *nor will they come to mind.*' 'Not be remembered' refers to conscious contents of memory, 'come to mind' to memories suddenly aroused. This verse suggests that not only will God blot out the past, but so shall we. All the past troubles of this life, all the failures, all the pangs of conscience which disturb us now will not even come to *our* minds then, let alone to God's to accuse us.

Although we can't imagine it (and who can fully imagine any of this?), such selective amnesia which applies to the old order of things must include those who, because of their refusal to embrace Christ's offer of salvation, are banished from his presence in Hell. Though such thoughts trouble us now, and so spur us on to pray for them and seek to share the gospel with them, they will not trouble us in the new world – such thoughts about the lost will simply not exist because such memories as they are will not exist. Instead, our memories will be reshaped and minds taken up in the adoration of God, basking in the great new works of his creative power, 'Be glad and rejoice *for ever* in what I will create' (v. 18). For according to the Book of Revelation the one who stands in the centre of the heavenly Jerusalem is Christ, the Lamb who was slain, whose radiant presence will flood our hearts with liquid joy.

Service is freedom

Secondly, Heaven is a place where there is *freedom for service*: 'my chosen ones will long enjoy the work of their hands, they will not toil in vain' (v. 22b).

What word would you use to sum up Heaven? The word most people would use is 'boring'. George Bernard Shaw in his typically pugnacious way captured what most people think like this. He said, 'Heaven is conventionally conceived is a place so inane, so dull, so useless, so miserable that nobody would venture to describe a whole day in heaven, though plenty of people have described a day at the seaside.' I guess he is right. That is Heaven as it is *conventionally* conceived, as if all we will do all day is waft around on some cloud, clothed in a celestial negligee, strumming a golden harp. It has to be admitted that sometimes we as Christians have contributed to this caricature because we have not paid attention to what Scripture says, albeit in image form.

The Bible teaches that Heaven will be a place of rest, but that is not the same as inactivity. Revelation 14:13 speaks of believers as being 'blessed, for they rest from their labours'. But the context makes it clear that the labours from which they are now released are those of spiritual warfare, battling against the world, the flesh and the devil. Now it is a battle, then it will be over and we will be at peace. Heaven is a rest not from work, but from opposition and toil.

Therefore, while there will be rest in Heaven there will also be activity in Heaven as is hinted at here with these pictures, we shall labour and unlike on earth there will be full satisfaction in our labours, the results won't disappoint us, either because we fail or someone else cuts in and reaps the benefits. Neither is work marred by pain or struggle. In Genesis 1 and 2 it is clear we were created to work, to serve God as his vice-regents. In the new heaven and earth that purpose will be perfectly realised. There our human powers will be at full stretch, as renewed by grace and made perfect in love, they serve God in Christ. Remember the parable of the talents in Matthew 25:14-30? There it is hinted that our responsibilities in the kingdom to come will increase or decrease according to the faithfulness we show now. As the great American theologian Jonathan Edwards put it so beautifully: 'In heaven it is directly the reverse of what it is on earth; for there, by length of time things become more and more youthful, that is more vigorous, active, tender, more beautiful.' Here we grow old, there we as it were grow young. Here our powers fade, there they increase. Heaven is not a habitation of transparent spirits, it is a city of people, remade in God's image for his service.

Babylon in perspective

Doesn't all of this put our present in some sort of context? What is it that we are investing in and putting our energies towards? What really matters? Ten billion years into eternity, how will that new hi-fi or kitchen, which at the moment is your pride and joy, appear then? After you have been caught up in the great celebration of the wedding feast of the lamb for twenty-five billion years, what will that struggle you have had as a Christian seem then? Those thoughts of giving up because it is too tough, or free-wheeling and trying to have the selfish hedonism of this life, spending most of our money on ourselves and throwing a few coppers into the collection plate – how do such thoughts and actions fare in the light of eternity?

It has never been easy for God's people living in 'Babylon'. But this world is not our final resting place – that is the world to come. So let us remember these words of Jesus as we seek to serve him where he has placed us, learning to travel light and never putting our roots down too deeply: 'I have told you these things, so that in me you may have peace. In this world you will have trouble. But take heart! I have overcome the world' (John 16:33).

Further Reading

Harry Blamires, *The Post Christian Mind* (Vine Books, 1999)

Harry Blamires, *Where Do We Stand?* (SPCK, 1980)

Charles Colson, *Against the Night* (Vine Books, 1999)

Os Guinness, *Time for Truth* (IVP, 2000)

Os Guinness, *Fit Bodies, Fat Minds* (Hodder, 1995)

Paul Helm, *The Last Things* (Banner of Truth, 1989)

Peter Hitchens, *The Abolition of Britain* (Quartet, 1999)

H. Jones, *Alfred. C. Kinsey: A Public Life* (Norton, 1997)

Tony Payne and Phillip Jensen, *Pure Sex* (Matthias Media, 1998)

J. Satinover, *Homosexuality and the Politics of Truth* (Baker, 1996)

C. Socarides, 'How America Went Gay' in *The Journal of Human Sexuality*.

Philippa Taylor, *For Better or For Worse* (CARE. 1998)

Kevin J. Vanhoozer, 'The Bible – Its relevance Today', in *God, Family and Sexuality*, ed, David. F. Torrance (Handsel Press, 1997)

David F. Wells, *God in the Wasteland* (IVP, 1994)

David Wright, *The Christian Faith and Homosexuality* (Rutherford House, 1994)